Tales of Old C

C000262238

Other counties covered by the *Tales* series include:

Berkshire
Buckinghamshire
Cambridgeshire
Cheshire
Cornwall
Cumbria
Derbyshire
Devon
East Anglia
Essex
Hampshire
Hertfordshire
Kent
Lincolnshire
Middlesex
Norfolk
Northamptonshire
Northumberland
Nottinghamshire
Oxfordshire
Shropshire
Somerset
Staffordshire
Suffolk
Sussex
Warwickshire
Wiltshire
North Yorkshire

Tales of Old County Durham

Martin Dufferwiel

Illustrations by Simon Jardine

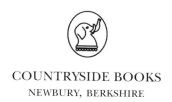

COUNTRYSIDE BOOKS
NEWBURY, BERKSHIRE

First published 2011
© Martin Dufferwiel, 2011

All rights reserved. No reproduction
permitted without the prior permission
of the publisher:

COUNTRYSIDE BOOKS
3 Catherine Road
Newbury, Berkshire

To view our complete range of books,
please visit us at
www.countrysidebooks.co.uk

ISBN 978 1 84674 249 1

For my family

Designed by Peter Davies, Nautilus Design
Produced through MRM Associates Ltd., Reading
Typeset by Jean Cussons Typesetting, Diss, Norfolk
Printed by Cambridge University Press

Contents

MAP OF OLD COUNTY DURHAM

Gateshead

South Shields

Sunderland

Consett

Chester-le-Street

Rookhope

Durham Dales

Weardale

Durham

Hetton Colliery

Wolsingham

Crook

Spennymoor

Middleton-in-Teesdale

Whitworth

Kirk Merrington

Hartlepool

Bishop Auckland

Sedgefield

Aycliffe

Brafferton

Barnard Castle

Darlington

N

Introduction

The county of Durham has its origins in that part of northern England that once made up the Patrimony of St Cuthbert, the great Anglo-Saxon saint, whose body was brought to Durham at the founding of the city in AD 995. Following the Norman invasion of 1066, those lands gradually evolved into the medieval County Palatine of Durham, power base of individuals in whom were invested the twin roles of Bishop of Durham and Count Palatine, and who are known popularly today as the Prince Bishops of Durham.

Such a long history inevitably gives rise to many stories – tales of events and of individuals – which have been thought worthy of recollection and have been written down over the course of those thousand years. Hopefully, therefore, in the re-telling of these tales, the reader will find much that is of interest in this little book. Stories are included from across the county: from Sunderland to the High Fells of Weardale, and from Darlington to the banks of the River Tyne at Jarrow.

But wait! I hear the murmuring reproachful voices of those who would now take issue. 'Ah,' they say, 'but some of these places are no longer in the County of Durham!' And of course, I must concur. But in writing this book I have taken as my geographical boundaries, the historical borders of County Durham. From the River Tyne in the north, to the River Tees in the south; from the North Sea coast in the east, to the far west, where the remotest reaches of the Durham Dales meet the lonely, windswept North Pennines.

Throughout the text I have quoted, quite liberally, from a number of Durham's renowned 18th- and 19th-century antiquarians and historians. By way of reference and acknowledgement to them and others, and for the benefit of readers who may wish to discover more of the history and traditions of old County Durham, a select bibliography of their works is included at the end of the book.

Martin Dufferwiel

The Pickled Parson

The word 'tithe' is Old English in origin. It means a tenth part of something. A tenth part of something that was, for almost a thousand years, contributed by parishioners to support the Church and the clergy. What you contributed depended on what you produced. It could be a tenth of your annual crop, a sack of wheat, a load of hay or a tenth of your newborn livestock; and it formed a significant part of the 'living' of a country parsonage.

Needless to say it was never popular with local farmers and they were often known to try and cheat their incumbent cleric, sometimes even resorting to killing the tenth animal of a litter or a brood. There were some vicars, however, who would not, and some who could not be cheated; they knew exactly what was due to them.

The vicar of Kirk Merrington, for example, was notorious for insisting on his tenth of everything. Every tenth stook of corn, every tenth pig from a litter, and so on. A local farmer once congratulated himself on eluding the eye of the covetous cleric after successfully raising a good brood of ten geese. Much later, however, when the birds were grown and fat, the vicar and his men arrived at the farm to claim his bird. The disappointed farmer, on asking the vicar why he had waited until now to claim his tenth, was told: 'I waited until it was ready.' And when a woman from Ferryhill gave birth to her tenth child, her husband suggested that perhaps they should give it to the vicar, saying: 'Ye knaa he tak's a tithe of iverything.'

The Reverend John Garnage, however, would undoubtedly have drawn the line at babies. He had come to the 13th-century church of St Edmund in the parish of Sedgefield in 1727, and had for twenty years ministered to the needs of its parishioners. An avuncular cleric, Garnage was popular, both with the villagers and with the local farmers. Always seen out and about, he was very much part of this rural community. Even so, the popular rector always took his annual tenth.

It was December 1747, the winter weather had taken a turn for the worse and Tithing Day was set for the 20th day of the month. The

rector had not been seen about the village for some time. Rumours spread that all was not well with him but Mrs Garnage was quick to allay the concerns of the parishioners. He was well enough, she said, a chill, that was all, probably caught during the recent bad weather. He was still about his business, she assured them, preparing, she reminded them, for the upcoming collection of the tithes.

As you would expect, for a popular man, neighbours called at the rectory to pay their respects to the Rev Garnage. However, his wife simply gestured in the direction of a private room in which the rector was recuperating, before hurriedly ushering the well-wishers away. He simply needed solitude and rest, she explained. His parishioners, though rather curious, ceased to be concerned.

The appointed day arrived and still the rector had not been seen. He was, according to his wife, still a little unwell and of course extremely busy with his annual collection. But the tithes were delivered regardless. The Tithe Barn was filled with the produce of the local farms and tenants called at the rectory with their rents. Met at the door by the rector's wife and conducted through the large and draughty old building to deposit their dues, they were unable to speak to the friendly old parson; he was still unwell but reclining peacefully in his quiet, darkened room. So they simply hailed their good wishes as they passed, but the lack of any response from the normally cheery cleric concerned them.

So the Tithing Day ended and the villagers had, for another year, performed their time honoured duty to the Church. The rector's wife had 'received the emoluments of the Living' on behalf of her sick husband and everyone's thoughts now turned to Christmas. But the next day the villagers heard the news that some of them had feared. The rector's wife announced, with great sadness, that her husband had not after all recovered from his illness; he had suddenly deteriorated and had departed this world.

Suspicions were immediately aroused, an investigation followed and the folk of Sedgefield were shocked to hear that the Rev Garnage had indeed died, but he'd been dead for two weeks!

If there was no incumbent clergyman, then the tithes due to that parish would go to the Bishop of Durham and the already extremely wealthy 'Fat Man of Auckland' would become even richer. This had been the motive for the extreme actions of the scheming, but poor, rector's wife. Fearing that this essential annual income would be lost to her after her husband's death, she had salted his body and hidden it in the very room into which the well-wishers had hailed their greetings; until the due day had come and gone and she had received her annual tenths. The tithes successfully collected, she had moved her husband's salted body back into his bed, cleaned it and claimed that he had died peacefully during the night.

In life, the rector of Sedgefield was no doubt an honourable and pious man. For in death it seems that his soul became displeased with the deception that had been carried out. John Sykes, writing in 1840, tells in his *Local Records* that the apparition of the now irreverently but alliteratively-named Pickled Parson soon began to infest the environs of the church and the rectory at Sedgefield, and for the best part of half a century terrified all the inhabitants by 'making night hideous'.

The original rectory house of the Rev J. Garnage, the 'Castellated Edifice' of the Pickled Parson of Sedgefield, was eventually destroyed in 1792, when a fire broke out in one of the lodging rooms – it is perhaps to be wondered whether it was the same room that had served as a quiet repose for his dead but still profitable body – and the whole building was burned down. With that, some say, the haunting ceased. A fine new hall, Ceddesfield Hall, was later built on the site of the original rectory.

With the introduction of the Tithe Commutation Act of 1836, the right to receive tithes, which had been introduced into England by King Aethelwulf in AD 855, was finally ended. But the ghost of the Pickled Parson of Sedgefield is still rumoured to haunt a lost tunnel – isn't there always a lost tunnel! – leading from St Edmund's church to the site of his own former rectory, where his salted corpse ensured that for the year 1747 the annual tithes due were definitely collected.

She Was Only the Postmaster's Daughter

Everyone likes a good romance. Some want only a happy ending but for others it is perhaps a bittersweet story of lost love that is most poignantly remembered.

Mr Clement, the postmaster of Darlington, was not at all sure that the romance that is the subject of this tale could ever work out happily. The story is set in the first half of the 18th century. Mr Clement was a respectable man but not a rich one. His salary of forty pounds a year was stretched thinly across his large family and he found it difficult to support them all.

So it was with great sadness that he arranged for his daughter Mary to enter into employment with the proprietor of a linen merchant's shop in London and off the girl was sent to begin her new life. The shop was run by a Mrs Rennie, a respectable lady, who, with the assistance of several other young women, saw to the day-to-day duties of attending to the needs of customers, especially the young society gentlemen who would come into the shop to procure the latest fashionable items for their wardrobes.

A regular customer at the shop was young Sir Edward, who, around the year 1730, had returned from his own Grand Tour of the Continent, to live in a fine house in Pall Mall. Sir Edward was the epitome of the fashionable young man about town. A dazzling figure, he would captivate the young shop girls with the many stories of his adventures in Europe. He was cultured, sophisticated, wealthy, well connected and handsome. And, so the chronicles tell, 'very engaging was he found by the ladies'.

To Mary, the young girl recently arrived from Darlington, Sir Edward was a world away from anything she had previously known and she was drawn to him like a moth to a flame. Though Mary was described as being 'as beautiful as an Angel', she was not versed in the culture and manners of high society; nonetheless, it appears that Sir Edward was in turn drawn to Mary. On his frequent visits to Mrs Rennie's establishment, it was always Mary that he sought out and a close friendship developed between the two. Sir Edward soon noted, with some sympathy, Mary's situation: her parents, with the rest of their large family still to support, were unable to help her. No money arrived for her from Darlington, no presents of clothes. So it was that Sir Edward himself began bringing presents to Mary, 'in a way not to alarm the vigilance of her mistress, who exacted the strictest morality from the young persons under her care' and their close friendship began to develop into something more. Needless to say, this did not go unnoticed by the good Mrs Rennie.

For Mrs Rennie, it seems, was fond of Mary Clement, who in her opinion was honest, decent and a good worker, and the benevolent employer began to have deep concerns about the developing liaison. The worldly-wise woman realised what Mary did not: that a relationship between two people from such completely different social backgrounds could never be. The gulf was too wide to be crossed decently and she feared for the young girl's reputation. Eventually she became so alarmed about the blossoming romance that she sent word to Darlington, to inform Mr Clement.

So it was that the Darlington postmaster arrived in London to remove his beloved daughter from 'that vortex of temptation'. It is said that he had tears in his eyes as he told her of Mrs Rennie's suspicions and of his own concerns. He had come to take her home, where she might still meet and marry 'some decent tradesman'. Mary pleaded her innocence and begged him to allow her to stay, explaining to him that Sir Edward was a friend and nothing more. Her father prevailed, however, and the distraught Mary eventually agreed to pack her things, empty her room and return north with him to Darlington.

As he waited, Mr Clement sat before the fire, in deep discussion with Mrs Rennie about the tragic but nonetheless necessary resolution of the situation. And Mary made her move. Without cloak or bonnet she ran from Mrs Rennie's establishment and made her way, pell-mell, to Pall Mall and the grand home of Sir Edward. After frantically knocking on the front door, she was told by the porter that the master was not at home, but 'as he knew her' he admitted her to the house in Sir Edward's absence. A distraught Mary was shown into the parlour, where the table had been set for dinner, there to await the return and the reaction of Sir Edward. She didn't have long to wait before she heard the front door being opened and after a hushed discussion with the porter, Sir Edward entered the room, looked across at Mary, and exclaimed, 'You, here!' At that, the rest of the servants were dismissed and whatever conversation passed between the young couple would never be known. But what is recorded is that Mary Clement, the postmaster's daughter from Darlington, 'Sat down that day, at the head of his table, and never left after it.'

So it was that Mary Clement and the young Sir Edward would eventually have four children, three girls and a boy. They never married, though they wanted to. For Sir Edward was Sir Edward Walpole, a younger son and one of the six children of the famous Whig statesman Sir Robert Walpole, generally regarded as the first Prime Minister of Great Britain, although that official title did not exist in his day. By his family connections alone, young Edward had a bright political career before him and thus Sir Robert at once forbade any marriage; a decision from which he would never relent. When Mary died giving birth to their fourth child and only son, it is said that Edward was devastated as he had been devoted to her and to their children. He never married. And from Mary's death it is said that, apart from pursuing his political career, he gave up the rest of his life to the education of his children and to the provision of his great affection, and necessities when needed, to Mary's family in Darlington.

There is an interesting footnote to the story in that, as it is recorded in the chronicles, Mary and Edward's second daughter, Maria, became by her first marriage Lady Waldegrave. Then, following her husband's untimely death, she married again, this time becoming part of the British royal family when, on 6th September 1766, she married Prince William Henry, Duke of Gloucester and Edinburgh, a younger brother of King George III (he was also an ancestor of the late Diana, Princess of Wales). And so it was that Maria went on to live a life of royal privilege, having her official portraits painted by both Reynolds and Gainsborough.

As well as her daughter, three of Mary Clement's grandchildren would be brought up as members of the British royal family: Princess Sophia Matilda, Princess Carolina Augusta Maria and Prince William Frederick. Some years later, a 19th-century chronicler mused: 'And hence it came within the bounds of probability, that the descendants of the Postmaster of Darlington, might one day have swayed the British Sceptre.'

Silver Buckles
at His Knees

T his is the story of a familiar song, a song about unrequited love
and heartless abandonment, or perhaps it isn't.

You may indeed have heard the ditty, for it is *Bonny Bobby Shafto*,
often recited as the children's nursery rhyme *Bobby Shafto's Gone to
Sea*; the story of how the titular hero of the tale, before leaving for
unknown maritime adventures and perhaps fame and fortune,
promises his lady love that they will be wed on his return.

The Shafto family had its origins in the Northumberland
borderlands and the familiar tune is thought to have originally been
written for the Northumbrian pipes. One of its earliest known
versions appeared in a music manuscript written in 1695, the name
of the tune then being *Brave Willy Forster*. But today, the place most
familiarly associated with *Bonny Bobby Shafto* is in County Durham, at
Whitworth Hall, near Spennymoor. The Whitworth estate was already
an ancient one when the Shaftos came to settle there around 1652.
Then the Hall was described as being a 'magnificent country
mansion', surrounded by thick woodland with its own deer park,
which survives to this day.

Bobby Shafto himself was born in 1732 and brought up at
Whitworth, the son of John Shafto, the Tory Member of Parliament
for Durham. Educated at Westminster School and Balliol College,
Oxford, Bobby had everything going for him: heir to a large and very
valuable estate, intelligent, good looking and witty, he was very much
part of the 'social set' and in demand amongst the rich and well
connected of 18th-century County Durham. When still in his
twenties, he had his portrait painted by Sir Joshua Reynolds. In it, he
stands proudly resplendent in the latest fashionable dress, a scarlet
frock coat, with black velvet collar and matching scarlet waistcoat, all
with gold fastenings and trim and a white lace shirt. Tall, fair-haired,

slim and youthful, he was perhaps something of a contrast to many other portrait subjects of the time.

One in particular who, it was said, was hopelessly smitten by Bonny Bobby's charms was the equally alliteratively-named Bridget Belasyse, of Brancepeth Castle, just across the River Wear from Whitworth. However, it seems that her hopeful affections were not reciprocated and Bobby spent his youth in the traditional pursuits of the landed gentry: shooting, fishing, riding to hounds and socialising. Eventually becoming involved in the politics of the day, he was almost thirty years of age when, in 1760, he followed in his father's footsteps and stood for Parliament. His opponent was the wealthy and powerful Whig politician Sir Thomas Clavering. However, Bobby too had influential friends and was supported in his campaign by both the Earl of Darlington and the Bishop of Durham. Bobby was triumphant and eventually took his place as a Member of Parliament, an occupation that would employ his time for the next eight years.

Popular tradition has it that the song *Bonny Bobby Shafto* was written by the lovestruck and ultimately tragic Bridget Belasyse, always dreaming, if perhaps not believing that *'He'll come back and marry me'*. Of course Bobby would have known Bridget. After all, in landed estate terms they were neighbours; they would mix in the same social circles and Bobby's younger brother, Thomas, was also the rector of Brancepeth, the parish in which Bridget and her widowed father lived. However, there seems to be no record of any reciprocal affection on his part, still less of any promise of marriage. But Bridget, it is said, began to become more and more obsessive about their clearly one-sided relationship. The story is told that she became so concerned about Bobby's 'socialising' that, perhaps a little bit sinisterly, as a surrogate stalker, she would despatch her page every day across the River Wear, to climb the bank that led to Whitworth Hall, there to spy on Bobby's comings and goings. Indeed, the scene of Bridget's agent's secret reconnoitring afterwards became known as Page Bank.

But gradually Bobby's lifestyle took him away from Whitworth more and more, away from prying, spying eyes and away from Bridget. And in the end, he never did come back to marry her, for in London, on 18th April 1774, he married Anne Duncombe, an heiress to large estates in Yorkshire and a much younger woman than Bridget. His brother Thomas officiated at the wedding. The sad tale tells that, after hearing news of the forthcoming marriage, Bridget Belasyse simply began to pine away until, just two weeks before the wedding,

aged thirty-eight, she died of a broken heart, although the tuberculosis she is thought to have contracted may have had more to do with her untimely demise.

The song *Bonny Bobby Shafto* with which we are familiar today was, it seems, used as an election jingle for Bobby's 1760 campaign and over the years different writers added new words and further verses to it, mostly alluding to Bobby's ongoing life and career. So you could say that Bonny Bobby was elected to Parliament mainly through the backing of powerful friends and a catchy tag line, proving perhaps that not all is new in the world of politics.

But Bobby's Parliamentary career was, as far as can be established, fairly nondescript and indeed the rest of his life passed without any particular distinction on his part. He simply lived, from what is known, the comfortable, well connected life of an 18th-century country squire. It is probably fair to say that whilst, in all other respects, Bonny Bobby Shafto, the hero of the tale, would have been lost to historical obscurity, the song about him has since taken on a life of its own.

The great 19th-century historian of Durham, Robert Surtees, tells us that in his day Brancepeth Castle was troubled by the restless haunting of a Grey Lady. It was thought that the spectre was the sad shade of Bridget Belasyse, still waiting for her Bonny Bobby to come back and be her own '*for evermair*'. But, contrary to popular belief, Bridget did not write the song *Bonny Bobby Shafto* and it can only be guessed at how she would have felt if, already spurned by the object of her love, the Durham 'society' of her day had sniggered at the rumour that she had.

In fact, there is some doubt as to whether the song refers to our Bobby at all – with a Northumbrian knight of the same name but of a different age, being a possible alternative hero. The Bobby Shafto of our story died in November 1797 and was buried in the family crypt under Whitworth church. He had held the Whitworth estate for fifty-five years, and he never did go to sea.

The Valour of
Earl Uchtred

A picturesque 16th-century poem entitled *To the Citye of Duresme*, written by Richard Cavendish in the year 1573, sings the praises of the once martial reputation of St Cuthbert's city, and in its lines refers to a singular incident that occurred at the beginning of the 11th century. The incident was to prove a precursor of the seemingly endless succession of attacks and sieges by Scottish armies, which would, over subsequent centuries, become such an alarming and regular feature of Durham's history.

They of thy Skordge have tasted oft; thy strengthe and hastye hande,
Caust Scottish King to lose his crowne, and barons of his land;
Thy marquet with their murders filled, thy gates and walles with heads,
Their bodyes in thy streats lay strawed, o town of doughty deeds.

The year was 1006. For almost three decades, England had been subjected to the weak and ill-advised rule of King Ethelred. Waltheof was the Earl of Northumbria; but he was old, infirm, confined to his stronghold of Bamburgh and, crucially, he was physically incapable of leading his own armies in the defence of his northern lands. This was now left to Uchtred, his son and heir apparent, himself a bold and resourceful warrior, who, in carrying out his loyal duties to his aged father, was beginning to establish his own reputation as a potent military leader. The Earls of Northumbria at Bamburgh had strong connections with the guardians of the Shrine of St Cuthbert at Durham; indeed, Uchtred had taken as his wife, Ecgfrida, the daughter of Aldhune the Bishop, reinforcing his position as both powerful and influential, heir to the Earldom of Northumbria and kin by marriage to the Church of Holy St Cuthbert and the see of Durham. Eleven years previously, the Northumbrians had helped the monks prepare the site for their first church and settlement and since the Community of St Cuthbert had been resident on the high wooded rock of the Dun Holme, the peninsula, already naturally surrounded and protected by the River Wear, had, with Uchtred's assistance, been cleared and further fortified against the unwelcome attention of those who jealously eyed it.

Malcolm II was King of Scotland and he was well aware of the unstable and uncertain military situation in England. Danish raiders were causing major problems for King Ethelred – for Ethelred was never really ready. Pacification and pay-off were his twin weapons against the Viking threat, weapons that the Danes were at first only too happy to face. So it was that the King's eyes were turned away from the distant north when Malcolm seized his chance and marched his army south. They swept through Northumberland, for the aged Waltheof, safe behind the walls of Bamburgh, was unable to challenge them. On, Malcolm's army came, unmolested until 'Having devastated the province of the Northumbrians with the sword and fire, he laid siege to Durham'. Here he meant to starve the population into submission and take the stronghold for his own.

Uchtred sent messengers to Ethelred, appealing for military aid but none could be given. Good fighting men were needed in the south, to stand for the King against the Danish foe. Most of those left in the north had seen too many battles, or too few. He appealed to Elfhelm, the powerful Ealdorman of York, but still no help came. In the end, to save the city of Durham, the Community of St Cuthbert and probably his own earldom, Uchtred sent messengers out across the wild lands of Northumbria and even down into Yorkshire, to muster whatever forces he could to stand against the Scots. So it was that the fighting men who had remained in their native lands rallied to his banner and he was able to assemble a hastily-pulled together, but nonetheless effective, fighting force, which, without further delay, advanced upon Durham to cut off any Scots' withdrawal and raise the siege.

Malcolm was caught unawares. He had wrongly assumed that the north of England had been emptied of fighting men to reinforce Ethelred's army in the south. The besieger now became the besieged; the predator had become the prey. No doubt, the monks of St Cuthbert, watching the unfolding life or death drama from their lofty vantage point, looked out across the River Wear towards the two opposing forces in fear and in hope, and with prayers for the victory of their earthly saviours. Uchtred gave the signal and the Northumbrians smashed against the massed lines of the Scottish besiegers.

The struggle was bitter and bloody but eventually Uchtred's men had the dominance 'and cut to pieces, nearly the entire multitude of the Scots'. At the end of the fighting, the field belonged to Northumbria; the Scots were routed and put to flight. The valour of Uchtred had won the day and his skill in battle and fighting spirit had won him his sobriquet. From that day on he would be known by all as Uchtred the Bold. King Malcolm escaped the carnage, managing to flee the battlefield and make his way back to Scotland with some of his closest allies. So the siege was raised and the infant city saved, but Uchtred decided that an example was needed to deter any further aggression, a warning to all who dared to threaten the independence of St Cuthbert's people and the Earldom of Northumbria that would surely now become his.

So it was that he ordered the 'best' heads of the slain Scottish warriors, 'ornamented, as was the fashion of the time, with braided locks', be cut off, collected and taken into Durham. There, tall poles were erected in the Market Place and all around the city walls and upon the poles were stuck the heads of the defeated dead, their lifeless eyes staring out as a dire warning to any others who might have shared their lost ambitions and who would certainly share their fate.

In an acknowledgement of his notable victory over the Scots, King Ethelred confirmed the Earldom of Northumbria upon Uchtred and added to it the Earldom of York, after having Elfhelm murdered for his refusal to send aid to Durham. Thus, the new Earl of Northumbria began what would be a short but illustrious military career; a career that would end only ten years later when he and forty of his men, on route to a meeting with King Cnut, were ambushed and slain by a band of Vikings.

Over the centuries to come, the Scots would, of course, be back many times; indeed, familiar would be the days when the suburbs of Gilesgate, Elvet and Framwelgate were lit by the light of Scottish fires. But for now, the city of Durham was saved and over five and a half centuries later, Richard Cavendish would have the material for his poem. It is told that the heads of the unfortunate Scots, before their spiking and display on the ramparts of 11th-century Durham, were given to four old dames of the city, who were charged with the task of washing the faces and combing the hair. For their gruesome labours, the no doubt eternally grateful old women were each presented with the invaluable gift of a cow.

How Pollard Won His Lands

Like the rest of medieval England, the County Palatine of Durham was home to large tracts of ancient woodland and the Prince Bishop's hunting forest of Weardale was second in size only to the King's own New Forest. But the dense green woodland was home not only to the King's, or even the Bishop's deer, but was also infested with the fearsome wild boar. Two of these creatures, the great Brawn of Brancepeth and the Felon Sow of Rokeby, have achieved legendary status. But there was another which, though feared throughout the beech and oak woods encircling the Bishop's Palace of Auckland, remained, at least for a time, just a formidable specimen of that traditionally bad tempered and dangerous species. Nevertheless, it was a specimen that secured a bold and enterprising knight, land and inheritance, land that is still known by his name today.

'The muse may sing how in a northern wood in olden time, a bristled Brawn was seen.'

Word had been given out that those living in and around the forests of Auckland were being terrorised by a huge and aggressive boar. There was even rumour of a substantial reward being offered by the Prince Bishop to the one who could slay the fierce creature and make the woodland safe again. Many had tried but, as yet, none had succeeded. Until one day the challenge was taken up by the hero of our story, a young knight by the name of Pollard.

Pollard had given the matter some consideration. Those that had previously sought out the boar, and fought against it in open combat, had met only failure or severe injury. There must, thought Pollard, be a better way to achieve this particular quest. So, mounting his horse, he set off for the deep woodland and the lair of the dread beast. He was aware of the habits of the creature. It was known to follow its own trails through the forest, keeping to the areas where it could find the richest food and Pollard knew that wild boar were especially fond of beech mast.

Upon reaching a large beech tree, which stood hard by one of the tracks frequented by the animal, Pollard now put his plan into action. Securing his horse a safe distance away, he climbed the tree and shook down from its branches as much beech mast as he could, spreading on the woodland floor below a banquet for the beast. Then, he waited, safe in the spreading canopy.

He waited for some time and he was beginning to question his own wisdom, wondering if the boar would indeed pass this way and partake of the feast prepared for it, when suddenly it appeared beneath him. Huge, bristling, ill-tempered and bearing the scars of many battles, the beast gratefully began gorging itself. It ate and it ate, oblivious to anything around, or above, it. After a while, it slowed, satiated. It seemed that, after such a feast, the giant boar was becoming tired. Pollard's chance had arrived.

He grasped his sword and leapt down from the beech tree. He had the surprise. The boar had no time to charge and Pollard struck it with cruel blows. But not for nothing had the beast earned its reputation and, recovering its wits, it turned on its assailant and with sharp tusks, eager for blood, again and again, charged the knight. Again and again its charge was repulsed until at length Pollard, almost at the end of his strength, struck the telling blow. The giant Boar of Auckland was felled and, with a last desperate effort, Pollard delivered to it the coup de grace. The exhausted knight cut out the tongue of the defeated beast as a trophy of his victory and then fell in a swoon, wishing for sleep until his strength was restored and he could ride to Auckland Palace and the Bishop, there to display his prize and claim his reward.

Long he slept and, when he woke, exultation was displaced by despair. For unbeknown to him, another had followed the trail of the Boar of Auckland and had come across the scene of its final, fatal combat. Whether or not the intruder had taken Pollard for a dead man and left him, he had lifted up the carcass of the boar himself and sped to Auckland Castle. Pollard quickly followed and, upon arrival, reported his victory. But, he was told that the boar had been vanquished by another, who would have the reward. Infuriated by the theft and the loss of his prize, Pollard thought desperately of how he could persuade the prelate that he was the victor. And then he asked a servant to enquire of the Bishop as to whether the corpse of the beast was complete, did it still have its tongue. If the

answer was no, then he could prove that it was he who was its real conqueror.

Of course it was proved so. The other knight's claim was rejected and he was dismissed in dishonour. The Bishop was, naturally, enormously grateful for the service that Pollard had provided; he complimented both his ingenuity and his martial skills and wished health and blessings on his house. However, when Pollard raised the subject of a suitable reward for his valour, the Bishop was somewhat less than forthcoming.

During the interview, the prelate was eating dinner and he said to Pollard, rather disingenuously, that for his reward he could have all the land he could ride around before the meal was over. It seemed that, unlike the Bishop's repast, Pollard's reward would not be substantial. Nonetheless, for the little time that he had, the resourceful knight mounted his horse and spurred it on. But if the prelate congratulated himself on his clever riposte to Pollard's request for a reward, Pollard was cleverer. For he didn't gallop his horse wildly and breathlessly around the surrounding wooded acres, he simply mounted and jogged around the Bishop's Palace of Auckland and, on completing its encirclement, he returned to the Bishop to claim his prize. Rather than being enraged by the arrogance of the knight, the Bishop was impressed by the intelligence and boldness he had shown and offered, this time genuinely, to exchange his own palace for 'five hundred broad acres on the east side of the River Gaunless', close by Bishop Auckland.

It is recorded that these lands would be held in perpetuity by the Pollard family in exchange for the service of the presentation of a falchion, a ceremonial sword, to every new Prince Bishop of Durham, on his first entering 'Pollard's Lands'. Here we perhaps see the merging of one local legend with another, for a similar presentation was made to the new Prince Bishop, upon his first entering the bishopric, by the Lords of Sockburn. Their particular weapon had allegedly been used by an ancestor of the Conyers family to slay, in ancient time, a monstrous 'worme, dragoune, or fierie serpent', and so it was that in some versions of Pollard's story the giant wild boar he slew was magically, but incorrectly, transmogrified into the 'Pollard Worm'.

So that is how Pollard won his reward and though the Pollard family itself became extinct in the reign of Queen Elizabeth I, unto this day the lands given to the conqueror of the giant Boar of Auckland, are still referred to as 'Pollard's Lands'.

The Remarkable
Mr John Gully

Some might say that this account should not really be included in a collection of stories about Durham, because the subject was not a native of the county and indeed spent much of his long life elsewhere. This is true, of course. At least it is true to say that the subject did not hail from the County Palatine – but it is equally true that he did end his days in Durham and therefore probably justifies at least a small place in this small book.

If you visit the city today and make your way, like many others, up Saddler Street, in the general direction of the cathedral, you will eventually come to a place where the road forks. The right turn will take you up onto Palace Green and you will be met by the ancient majesty of the World Heritage Site. If, however, you keep on going straight, along what is the North Bailey, within a short distance you will see on your left-hand side, a large brick building, a kind of brownish, greyish colour, with small windows. It stands, surrounded by period buildings amongst which, some would probably say, it looks startlingly out of place; a testament perhaps to the glories of 20th-century architecture. If you look closely, you will see on the wall, overlooking the street, a small brass plaque which tells that on the site of this new building once stood the old house of one John Gully, who died here in 1863. So who was this man who, a century after his death, was thought worthy of remembrance in the city of Durham?

Actually, the remarkable Mr John Gully had not always lived in this house. On first moving to Durham, around 1860, he had bought Cocken Hall, not far from the city, for Gully was a wealthy man. He had made his money from investing in land and, more importantly, in a number of collieries in the vast County Durham coalfield, investments that had returned a healthy profit.

He had originally bought shares in Hetton Colliery at an advantageously low price, shares he later sold at a high premium. With his profit, he invested in new ventures, sinking collieries at Thornley, in the east of the county and maintaining his interest in them until eventually selling on for further profit. Later, he pursued an interest in collieries at Trimdon and Wingate Grange and these he still held, as sole proprietor, at his death. Of course, in order to be such a successful investor in coal mines, Gully needed in the first place to be wealthy enough to be able to lay out the significant amount of capital needed. And it is said that the money he laid down for his Hetton shares, he had obtained by winning a bet. For the remarkable Mr John Gully had not always been a colliery owner.

It has been suggested that the bet, of several thousand pounds, was laid down by 'a noble lord', to the effect that John Gully would not be victorious in his Parliamentary election campaign. The bet had been won when Gully was elected to Parliament in 1832, as a representative of the Earl of Mexborough and for the Borough of Pontefract. With his liberal views, he was a member of the reforming movement of the day and supported the extension of the franchise. Indeed, he attended the first meeting of the Reformed Parliament in 1833 and would sit as an MP for almost five years.

But Gully it seems was not ideally suited to life as a Member of the House of Commons and the speeches that he made were described as 'neither numerous nor brilliant'; though, perhaps in contrast to today's politicians, it was said that he always 'acted moderately and sensibly'. However, unlike some of his contemporaries at Westminster, he had not been born into the governing classes of the day and, just as the remarkable Mr John Gully had not always been a colliery owner, neither had he always been a politician.

What he had always been, however, was a keen sportsman. Gully had a sure eye for matters of the turf and what he had always enjoyed, and been very successful at, was gambling. In fact he had been so successful that he had accumulated enough money to buy his own large landed estates: first Hare Park in Hertfordshire, and later Ackworth Park in Yorkshire. With his success, his knowledge and his often lucrative advice, he became an accepted member of 'the first circles of the country on terms of intimacy and friendship', eventually even being presented at Court.

For a time Gully had a permanent home at Newmarket and he was well known as a racehorse owner and breeder of some distinction; beginning in a small way perhaps, but then, with the generous assistance of 'smiling fortune', moving on to greater things. Indeed, his success was such that he was appointed a principal betting agent for the Prince of Wales, later, King George IV. This, of course, led to more commissions from various moneyed noblemen and gentlemen connected with Newmarket.

But Gully had done far more than make money from betting, he had owned, either solely or in partnership, some of the finest racehorses of the day. And with a good deal of irony, it was because of the good humour and fortitude that he showed when, in 1827, at Doncaster, he lost £40,000 of his own money, that his racing and gaming profile became 'high amongst the most honourable members of the turf'.

But Gully didn't always lose. In 1832 his horse, which he jointly owned with his business partner, won the Derby, and £50,000. The same year Gully's own horse won the St Leger, and a prize of £35,000. Indeed, there were few racehorse owners of the time as successful as he became. In his racing career, his own horses won the Derby twice, and he had a half share in horses that won the same race on two different occasions. His success continued. He won the Oaks, the St Leger and the Two Thousand Guineas. Over the 1854 season, his horses won him over £10,500 in first-place prize money alone.

Although poorly educated, in character Gully was described as intelligent, kindly and good humoured and he would never hide nor be reluctant to discuss his humble origins. For the remarkable Mr John Gully had not always been a successful racehorse owner.

His preceding occupation had begun in Bristol. For this city, where Gully had been born, along with its neighbour and rival, Bath, to where he had moved as a boy, had a reputation for prizefighting. As a young man, Gully had always taken a keen interest in this brutal occupation and had to some extent 'fancied his chances'. And it was in Bristol that an encounter with the then English champion prizefighter, Henry Pearce, who may have been an acquaintance of the young man, would change Gully's life for ever and set him on his way to his own meteoric pugilistic career.

We are, of course, familiar today with the fact that it is deemed necessary for all boxers to possess a suitably menacing sobriquet; in Pearce's case, however, he was known by the curious and ambiguous epithet of the 'Bristol Game Chicken'. So it was that a 'set-to' was arranged between Gully and the Game Chicken. Gully was a natural athlete, well muscled and standing just under six feet tall, but totally inexperienced. Of course the champion was successful, but Gully acquitted himself well. Perhaps, it was thought, with the right guidance, he could seriously challenge Henry Pearce for the English championship, perhaps this was his future.

John Gully, the prizefighter was born and with the financial assistance of a number of influential backers, who recognised a potentially significant future return, he was taken and trained specifically to fight Pearce for the Championship of all England. And in this endeavour, we are told, he showed a confidence in his own ability 'and an infinite amount of pluck'.

So the day of the fight dawned, it was 8th October 1805, at Hailsham, Sussex. In front of a vast crowd of spectators with 'persons of Royal and Aristocratic rank being in full force', including the future King William IV, the two men fought and after sixty-four rounds of bare-knuckled battering, the young Gully was forced to yield. Both men had dreadful injuries with Gully almost blinded and Pearce saying at the end to his young opponent, 'You are a good fellow! I'm hard pressed to stand.' Later, to friends, Pearce admitted that it had been the hardest fight he'd ever had. As a prizefighter, Gully, it seemed, had everything: physique, strength, technical ability and a formidable fighting spirit.

Eventually, Pearce was forced 'by severe bodily illness' to retire and Gully, though uncrowned, was regarded as his rightful successor. He became famous, his reputation such that it was two years before anyone challenged him.

Eventually, a Lancastrian named Bob Gregson did. He was much bigger than Gully, standing six feet two inches 'and of prodigious strength'. He had made his reputation by winning a number of brutal encounters. The fight took place on 14th October 1807. The fortunes of the contestants fluctuated up until the twenty-third round, by which time the two men were incapable of holding up their hands in front of them and both collapsed to the floor at the end of each round. Gully eventually struck the winning blow in the thirty-sixth round, leaving Gregson needing medical assistance.

Gregson, the 'Lancashire Giant', was defeated but he soon challenged Gully to a rematch. The fight was to be for the undisputed championship and £250. It took place on 10th May 1808, at Sir John Sebright's park in Hertfordshire and it was reported that so many people suddenly descended that day to watch the fight that the locals, seeing in the distance the massed ranks of spectators coming their way, thought that the French had landed, and called out the Volunteers. So Gully and Gregson went at it again: bare knuckles, bare-chested, and in white breeches and silk stockings. Gregson was felled at the end of the first round but it took Gully another twenty-seven to finally finish the challenger off. The undisputed champion then put his outer clothing back on and told the referee and the leading patrons that he was retiring.

In his short career as a pugilist 'he had earned a niche in the temple of Pancratic fame', but now he had become the proprietor of a London tavern – this he thought was his future. For the remarkable Mr John Gully had not always been a prizefighter.

But it had been prizefighting that had lifted him from his former life. His father had been a butcher and the young John had followed him into the family business. When his father died, however, the business collapsed and the family were left with unpayable debts. So it was that, aged only twenty-one, John was in the debtors' prison when the visit to that establishment by Henry Pearce and the subsequent paying off of Gully's debts by moneyed supporters of the prizefighting game were to decide his destiny.

On 9th March 1863 John Gully died in his house in the North Bailey, Durham City, which stood on the site of its brownish, greyish, small-windowed replacement of today. He had lived to his eightieth year and left twenty-four children by two wives, having twelve children with each wife. The wording on today's plaque simply tells us that here stood the house of: 'John Gully M.P. 1783 to 1863; Prize Fighter, Race Horse and Colliery Owner'.

Of course the idea of a 'legislator and pugilist' is today perhaps a curious and unlikely one. However, it must be remembered that not so many years ago, a certain former amateur boxer and deputy prime minister, no less, hit more than the news headlines, when, on arriving at an election rally, he landed a well-aimed and, probably, deserved punch on an egg-throwing protestor.

A Warning to
the Covetous

Genius Loci (Latin) – The Guardian Spirit of a Place
(Oxford English Dictionary)

Have you ever been somewhere and become aware of an elusive but nonetheless undeniable atmosphere and said out loud to whoever you were with, or perhaps just to yourself in your own head, that 'This place has a nice feel!'? Or have you sometimes felt the intangible but nonetheless uncomfortable opposite, of something faintly but disquietingly negative, when, perhaps with a slight shiver, you suddenly realised that you really did want to leave and go elsewhere?

Such instincts can be felt in response to many things. Perhaps it is the sense of awe brought about by the overwhelming space of a vast and ancient cathedral, its atmosphere heavy with the weight of years. Perhaps it is the gentle, intoxicating babble of a stream or the buzzing of summer insects. Perhaps it is the swell of birdsong in billowing woodland or the reverential silence of a mountain top. Or perhaps it is something darker, more unnerving; the unknowable mysteries of a forbidding stone circle, or the black depths of a lonely wood in the night-time. But, whether pleasant and calming or forbidding and threatening, is there perhaps on these occasions something more at work than just the spirit of the place?

In the days before modern archaeology and its strictly academic and scientific approach to the physical historical record, with its 'stratigraphy', its 'geo-phys' and its rigorous application of present-day disciplines and technology, the study of the distant past was partly the preserve of 'gentlemen antiquarians'. Many of these were Victorian amateurs; most had money, social standing, and time on their hands. Some were well meaning and enthusiastic in their efforts to uncover the secrets of ages long gone and undoubtedly added to the historical record. Others perhaps were more attracted by the lure of the sensational or even by the possibility of hidden treasures in ancient graves.

Not far from Middleton in Teesdale, stands a high, lonely hill, crowned by a stand of pine trees. As a landmark it is well known, its name recorded variously down the years as Kirkcarrion, Kirk Arran, Kyr Arran and Carreg Caryn. Upon its summit, so it was said, was the burial place of a Bronze Age chieftain named Caryn and, for millennia, there he had lain, undisturbed in his hallowed spot.

Around the year 1804, however, permission was given by the landowner for excavations to be carried out at Caryn's legendary resting place. Ostensibly the operation was to extract stone to be used for the enclosure of nearby pastureland and to build moorland walls on the slopes of Harter Fell, but it was also decided to take the opportunity to investigate the story of the ancient grave. Was it really there? And if it was, what might it contain?

So the work commenced and a team of about a dozen workmen under the supervision of an unknown antiquarian – or more likely, according to some, under the orders of Lord Strathmore's bailiff – began robbing the site of its layers of stony protection. After long hours of digging and clearing there was sudden excitement when what appeared to be a stone coffin was revealed. What, it was wondered, was hidden inside it: gold, jewellery perhaps, or the treasures of a time long since past? With great curiosity, and perhaps no little trepidation, the men began, very gradually, to lift the great covering slab of stone that had kept its contents, or its occupant, hidden from the world for so many ages of man.

After much heaving, sweating and struggling, the lid of the coffin was at last lifted and cast aside. The permanent darkness of over three millennia was burned away in an instant as the sunlight poured in, finally exposing the contents, which were lit up for all who were there to see. What they did see was a large pottery urn, unbroken and untouched by human hand since it had been placed in the tomb so many centuries before. What riches, they wondered, did it contain?

Later writers have told us that what in fact they had discovered was a kistvaen burial from the Middle Bronze Age, around 1400 BC. A kistvaen, or simply kist, is a rectangular, coffin-shaped chamber, normally made up of four or more large slabs of stone, each set on edge, with a fifth laid on top of them to act as a lid. The pottery urn that their eyes had fallen upon was a round, cinerary urn, which had been used by those far distant ancestors to contain the cremated remains of a chieftain or other individual prominent in their society.

And so, the excited men gazed with growing curiosity into the now fully exposed kist. But very soon, excitement and curiosity gave way to avarice. When all had gathered their breath and their thoughts, the lure of a lost fortune became too great. This may indeed have been the last resting place of Caryn himself but respect for the dead did not overcome the anticipation of hidden riches. The first of the diggers reached into the chamber and with an exclamation of 'It's aa'll mine', greedily grasped the urn and, in his frantic hurry to discover its secrets, straight away emptied it of its contents. Of course there was no treasure inside it, no gold or silver, and no 'jools'. What the men did see, however, suddenly made them question whether their selfish and greedy course of action had indeed been the wisest one. For when the ancient vessel was upturned, out of it came some strange dark material that they didn't recognise and something else that they did recognise – a blackened and shattered human bone. The rest was just ashes and dust, which was quickly cradled in the arms of the restless north wind and carried far away from that high place.

So, no treasure, no 'Wonderful Things', as were reported in the tomb of Tutankhamen. But, just as happened in that much later story, tales soon began to circulate of the alarming fate that seemed to have befallen those who had disturbed the ancient resting place of Caryn – stories of sudden deaths and a vengeful curse. It was reported that the man who had first reached into the kist to retrieve and empty its contents, soon after died a painful death in mysterious circumstances; and a ghostly apparition began to be witnessed on the top of Kirkcarrion, seemingly looking out across the vale, like some spectral watcher or guardian. Was it Caryn himself, returned from his sleep of ages to take revenge on those who had disturbed him, or was it perhaps some other vengeful spirit? No one knew, or dared to climb the hill to find out.

It seems that once the grave had been emptied and the stone cleared away, the site of this uncanny excavation was marked for posterity by the planting of a stand of trees. It also seems that where the urn and its contents were taken, ill fortune followed.

The 'treasure' of Kirkcarrion found its way to Streatlam Castle, near Barnard Castle, then the County Durham home of the Bowes family, who divided their time between Streatlam and their Scottish residence, Glamis Castle. The 18th-century Durham historian William

Hutchinson described the situation and appearance of Streatlam as 'gloomy and confined', situated, as it was, in the bottom of a deep valley, surrounded by about 400 acres of woodland. Writing sometime later, Sir Cuthbert Sharp tells of its 'quiet grandeur and solemnity', though admitting that 'it has evidently been chosen and retained from more imperious considerations than the smiling and picturesque beauty of the landscape'. And it seems that the contents of Caryn's tomb did little to lift the sombre mood and oppressive atmosphere at Streatlam. Over time, for whatever reasons, the house fell out of favour, and the once fine home began a long but terminal decline. The Bowes family decided to relocate their main residence to Glamis, and Streatlam Castle, where the finds of Kirkcarrion had been given a home, would eventually be deserted and was finally demolished in 1927.

Before its demise, however, most of the contents of Streatlam Castle were auctioned off. The remainder was carried away to Scotland, to Glamis Castle, famous for being the childhood home of Elizabeth Bowes-Lyon, the late Queen Elizabeth The Queen Mother; and probably equally, if not more famous, for being one of the most haunted castles in Britain. Perhaps the Kirkcarrion find now resides with the numerous unquiet spirits of Glamis Castle.

And perhaps the mysterious guardian still watches over the wooded hilltop. Over the years, there have been stories, whispers, of shadowy figures, sometimes seen standing in plain sight atop the hill; other times glimpsed out of the corner of an eye, fleetingly and unnervingly amongst the pine trees. It has been suggested that the strange, otherworldly atmosphere that some people say they have experienced there is present because the hill itself is situated on a ley line – one of those mysterious lines of power which, so those who propose such theories would have us believe, are perhaps a focus for mysterious earth energies or perhaps even for the lost magic of the ancients. Or perhaps it is a liminal place, where the boundaries between our world and some alternative world, or alternative reality, become blurred. It has even been said that on windy days there is always a place within the trees on the top of Kirkcarrion where no wind blows, no matter how it rages on the hillside.

No one really knows who it is that haunts Kirkcarrion. Perhaps it is Caryn himself, or perhaps the shades of his Bronze Age people, released into the modern world by the actions of those 19th-century workmen. Some have suggested it is the ghost of that unfortunate digger who, in life, was the first to plunder the grave and now pays in eternity for his avarice, tied for ever to the scene of his disrespect. It has even been said that it is the remorseful spirit of the landowner himself, who first gave permission for the ancient site to be disturbed. Perhaps indeed it is one or all of these restless spirits; or perhaps it simply is, and always has been, the *Genius Loci*.

Farewell Jobling

Hangings used to take place behind the high, secure, enclosed walls of Durham gaol, at least after 1869 they did. Previous to that, executions were carried out in public, in front of the prison and the court, the gallows platform set up above the main door of the court building.

A public hanging could attract a large crowd and though normally just a 'good day out' for the family, the notoriety of the crime, or the controversy of the trial or verdict, could influence the mood of the onlookers. Vengeful, remorseful or joyous, the citizens of Durham City on the day of an execution could expect to see anything from a street party to a riot.

On 3rd August 1832 the mood of the crowd was sombre and security was tight, as the onlookers gathered in Old Elvet. The condemned man was brought out to meet his fate. He stood straight and bore himself well. He moved as if to address the crowd, but his words failed him at the last and he could not. The rope was placed around his neck and, one by one, the bolts that held up the trap door upon which he stood were removed. Just as the final bolt was released, a voice from the crowd cried out 'Farewell, Jobling'. The condemned man turned his head in the direction of the cry and in doing so, displaced the knot in the rope. The last bolt shot back and he dropped but the rope did not now do its job of despatching him cleanly, with a broken neck, and instead of a 'short drop and a sharp stop', this unfortunate was doomed to the agonies of gradual strangulation.

The first quarter of the 19th century had brought years of political struggle for the working classes – a struggle both for social and electoral reform. The year 1819 saw the so-called Peterloo Massacre, when hundreds of peaceful protestors in St Peter's Field, Manchester were charged by the militia, on the orders of the Government, and innocent people were killed or injured. Riots, strikes, civil unrest, it was hoped by some in power that reasoned reform would offset the threat of revolution. It was feared by others that reform was simply revolution's infant child.

In County Durham the coal miners had been on strike for months and feelings between the miners and the colliery owners had become bitter and entrenched. Striking miners had been evicted from their homes by the owners and the pits where they worked were guarded at all times by the military. The Marquess of Londonderry, one of Durham's foremost colliery owners, had called a general meeting to try and persuade his miners to return to work, but they discovered that he had secretly brought with him, and held in reserve, a company of soldiers to strengthen his argument. Such was the threat.

In Jarrow a certain well-known magistrate named Nicholas Fairles had made himself notorious with his zeal in prosecuting the striking miners. On Monday, 11th June 1832 he had been riding by Jarrow Slake, on his way from Barnes Colliery to Jarrow Colliery 'in discharge of his Magisterial Duties', when he was recognised and accosted by two miners. They asked him for charity and when he refused, he was dragged from his horse. One of the men struck him a violent blow to the head with a brick. Unconscious and unable to defend himself, he was then beaten so badly by his assailant that the 71-year-old magistrate lay ten days before dying from his injuries.

The two men were instantly doomed, however, for the incident had been witnessed from the window of a nearby house. The murderers, it was said, had been recognised. One in particular, Ralph Armstrong, described in the warrant as 'a well known Pitman, about forty four years of age, late in the employment of Jarrow Colliery', was a notorious troublemaker and petty criminal, well known to the authorities. The man who was with him on that fateful day was 30-year-old Jarrow miner William Jobling. The alarm was quickly raised and Jobling was arrested the very same evening but Armstrong escaped.

At the subsequent coroner's inquest, the jury returned a verdict of wilful murder and a reward of £300 was offered for any information that would lead to the conviction of Jobling. A warrant was also issued for Armstrong's arrest, with a further £100 reward offered for anyone who could help bring him to justice.

In the meantime, the authorities ensured that Nicholas Fairles, the highly respected, or notorious, magistrate, had a send off befitting his station. On Wednesday, 27th June flags on church steeples and those on the ships in South Shields harbour were flown at half-mast, as a mark of respect, and most of the shops were closed for business.

As well as his family, a procession of notables followed him to his grave, including civic leaders, churchmen, fellow magistrates and other members of the legal profession, as well as the Chairman of the County Durham Quarter Sessions and, it is said, a large number of 'respectable householders'. No miners, it seems, joined in either the procession, or the mourning. However, there was general agreement amongst those of the establishment that an outrage such as this could not be tolerated. An attack on a member of the judiciary smacked of anarchy and to prevent something similar happening again, an example needed to be made.

It seemed, therefore, that for William Jobling, incarcerated and awaiting his trial, the omens were not good. So it was that his trial came and Jobling had his day in court. Throughout the proceedings Jobling contended that he was innocent of the crime and it had been Armstrong who had struck the magistrate the fatal blows. It seems that some of the witnesses supported what Jobling claimed. There was indeed a good deal of public sympathy for him; people who knew Jobling couldn't believe that he was capable of such a dreadful crime. Those who knew Armstrong, however, were convinced that he was. A general appeal was sent out to Armstrong, wherever he was, to hand himself in and save an innocent man from the gallows. But the appeal was ignored. William Jobling was found guilty of murder and sentenced to be hanged at Durham on Friday, 3rd August 1832.

Whilst awaiting sentence, Jobling, who could neither read nor write, asked friends to read to him from various books. Contemplating his own demise, he requested that certain lines from these books, which seemed to him particularly apposite to his situation, be written down. He requested of the prison authorities that these be copied out and distributed amongst the crowd before his execution. His request was denied and he was left to ponder the harsh reality, that if he wished to address the crowd, he would have to do so verbally. This he attempted to do, but failed.

There was a significant and perhaps dangerous level of support for Jobling, especially amongst the striking miners, and general agreement that Ralph Armstrong was the real culprit. Indeed, it had even been rumoured that the murdered magistrate had actually identified Armstrong as the killer. Jobling, it seems, had simply been in the wrong place at the wrong time. It was felt that he was unjustly being made the example that those in power demanded.

Because of the controversial circumstances surrounding Jobling's trial and sentence of death, the authorities had ordered a military presence at the execution and fifty mounted Hussars, together with fifty armed foot soldiers, lined up in front of the drop. There they remained, while the body was left to hang for an hour. In something of an unfortunate twist of fate for Jobling, a statute had recently been enacted which, perhaps in response to the general social unrest of the time, revived an old law that condemned any murderer to the gibbet. So it was that the lifeless body of William Jobling was taken down and pitched, in preparation for its grotesque final display.

It had always been the grim tradition that the bodies of executed murderers were gibbeted within sight of the scene of their crime. On the morning of Monday, 6th August, Jobling's body, along with a military escort, began its journey north, for it was to hang at Jarrow Slake, opposite the scene of the murder. When all was ready, the procession moved off, through Chester-le-Street, Picktree, White Mare Pool and then via the turnpike road to Jarrow. There, with a watchful guard of both cavalry and infantry, Jobling's pitched body was bolted into the iron cage that had been specially made to hold it, and at low tide was conveyed 'across the sludge to the Gibbett'. The gibbet itself, fixed into a stone weighing a ton and a half, which had been sunk deep into the mud, stood proud of the high water mark by fully seventeen feet, and there the body of William Jobling was left as an example for all to see.

However, on the night of 31st August, it disappeared. It was rumoured, though never proven, that a group of his fellow miners came under the cover of darkness, to that grim spot, and took his body down. Whatever happened to it, no one would ever say. It was said by some that it had been taken away and buried at sea, or, more poetically perhaps, that it had been carried off and buried under a wall of the Venerable Bede's old Jarrow monastery.

The statute, under which the unfortunate Jobling was gibbeted, was repealed just two years later and it is thought that he was the only person ever to be gibbeted under this particular Act. It has also been said that Jobling's gibbet on Jarrow Slake was, as a consequence of this, the last gibbet ever erected in England.

And so William Jobling was laid to rest, in whatever spot was chosen to be so. The £100 reward for the arrest and conviction of Ralph Armstrong, who most considered to be the real murderer of Nicholas Fairles, was never collected, for Armstrong was never seen again.

Humble Duck
– Cast Out!

There are no chiming bells or strange pantomime cats in this particular story, but there is a raven, and if the reader does note certain similarities with another story, please do not contact the author.

Nobody knew where he came from. Some have suggested that he was relatively local, possibly hailing from nearby Lumley. Others were not so sure. The noted 19th-century Durham antiquarian M.A. Richardson asserted that the origins and antecedents of the hero of this story 'remain veiled in impenetrable obscurity'. Anyway, in the middle years of the 17th century he found himself in Durham City, seeking employment.

So our hero, John Ducke, known to posterity as John Duck, had come to Durham City in search of work, potential fortune and perhaps a little fame. Unfortunately for Duck, England had just fought a vicious civil war, Oliver Cromwell was Lord Protector and England a republic. Strangers of any kind were viewed with suspicion. Had they stood for the King during the conflict or for Parliament? In addition, employment in the city of Durham at this time was controlled by the various trade guilds and unless you were, and remained, blessed with their authority, you would be cast out from the trade, from your employment and most likely from the city.

It has been suggested that Duck had previously been apprenticed to a butcher and, whether he had or not, this was the employment which he now sought. He was successful and was given an apprenticeship by a prominent city butcher by the name of John Heslop. For some time all went well; Duck worked diligently, quickly developed a sharp head for 'business' and, of course, fell in love with his employer's daughter. His happy situation was complete when, on 30th July 1655, John Duck married Anne Heslop in St Nicholas' church in Durham market place.

However, storm clouds were gathering. At a meeting of the Durham Guild of Butchers in January 1656, Heslop was reprimanded and warned 'to forebear to sett John Ducke on worke in the trade of Butcher, on paine of 39s.11d'. Pressure was placed on Heslop to release the apprentice from his employment. There were still suspicions about Duck's background and, to protect his own livelihood, Heslop was forced to let his son-in-law go. What to do now? Despondent, rejected, alone, Duck believed that he would have to depart from Durham to seek his fortune elsewhere, leaving behind him his new wife and a future until very recently so full of promise.

At this point in the story, fact blurs almost into fiction. For it is told that as Duck made his way along the banks of the River Wear, towards Framwellgate Bridge and the road out of the city, a raven flew overhead. Looking up, Duck caught a glimpse of a small object that slipped from the bird's beak and fell to earth, glinting in the morning sunlight as it did so. The unlooked for treasure fell at Duck's feet and picking it up he saw it was a gold coin, later described by the Durham historian William Fordyce, as 'A Fine Gold Jacobus'. Perhaps then, Duck's luck had turned again and, with this young man's finely-tuned business acumen, the golden seed had fallen into fertile soil.

Ruminating on his good fortune and what it meant, he noticed a cowherd driving his charges, with no little difficulty, across the bridge to Durham market. Perhaps this was an opportunity not to be missed and Duck, not failing to miss it, offered the unexpected bounty of his gold coin to the herdsman for a particularly fractious young calf. A coin worth 25 shillings was far too good an offer to pass up; it was gratefully accepted by the harassed cowherd and Duck turned again to the old city with the beginnings of a new career as a successful livestock trader. It was not long before the calf became a cow, which became a herd, and the butcher's boy began to grow very rich.

Like most successful entrepreneurs, John Duck began to develop a 'portfolio' of financial interests. As well as his livestock business, he invested his money in land and property, from which he collected rents. He also supplied mortgages, established, so it has been said, quite a profitable sideline in money-lending and took a keen interest in the burgeoning coal mining industry. It has also been suggested that some of his moneymaking enterprises were somewhat less wholesome than others. Indeed, there seems to have been a slightly 'shady' side to our hero, who, it has been claimed, was never averse

to foreclosing on mortgages or calling in loans, with no thought to the consequences of his actions. Nonetheless, over the course of the next twenty years, his fortune grew relentlessly and became considerable, and he was knighted by King Charles II.

We now return to pantomime territory. By 1680 the fortune of John Duck had grown to such an extent that he was able to purchase the nearby manor of Haswell on the Hill and surely the irony was not lost on him when he was invited to become a Freeman of the Durham Guild of Butchers. Then at last, in that same year, and in the best traditions of a good story, 'humble Duck cast out' was made Mayor of Durham.

In 1686, Duck the Money-lender turned Duck the Philanthropist when he endowed a hospital at Lumley 'for the sustentation and relief of twelve poor, aged and impotent people'. He became an alderman of Durham and then, on 19th March 1687, came his highest honour; he was created a baronet by King James II.

Always a staunch supporter of the Stuart monarchy, it has been suggested that former butcher's boy, Sir John Duck of Haswell on the Hill, rather sniffingly punned by later writers as 'Knight of the Cleaver', had lent money to the King, or to his profligate brother Charles II, and his baronetcy had been given to him in recognition of some singular service rendered to his royal patrons in that regard.

Even as he got older and wealthier, Sir John Duck, Bart of Haswell on the Hill, still had an eye for a profit. He pursued his interest in coal mines. From the Dean and Chapter of Durham, he took out leases at £22 per annum for the coal mines at Rainton, Moorsley and Moorhouse. More collieries would follow, and all were lucrative; indeed one particularly wealthy coal seam at Rainton colliery became widely known as 'Old Duck's Main'. Once more, Duck's luck had held.

So it was that two of the wealthiest citizens Durham had ever known – Sir John and Lady Anne Duck – eventually retired to a grand mansion built at the top of Silver Street in Durham City. If John Duck was blessed with material riches, though, he was not to be blessed with family. He and Anne were to remain childless, as an old rhyme relates:

> *On Duck the Butchers shut the door,*
> *But Heslop's daughter Johnny wed;*
> *In mortgage rich, in offspring poor,*
> *Nor son nor daughter crowned his bed.*

At the age of fifty-nine, his remarkable life came to an end at his Silver Street mansion, during the night of Wednesday, 26th August 1691. He was buried in the church of St Margaret of Antioch in Crossgate where, four years later, Lady Anne Duck, the plain Anne Heslop of all those years ago, would be laid to rest beside him. And today they lie there still.

After his death, all his estates, built up over a lifetime, were sold and dispersed. His Silver Street mansion eventually became an inn, known for years to townspeople as the Black Lion. When our hero died, his baronetcy died with him and the life and career of Sir John Duck, Bart of Haswell on the Hill, 'humble Duck cast out', passed away out of remembrance.

A room in his Silver Street mansion was adorned with a painted panel, a depiction of the luck of John Duck and the bizarre, if fortuitous, incident on Framwellgate Bridge. Whether the painting recorded a true moment of destiny or merely represented an apocryphal story, of John Duck himself there can be no doubt. The humble butcher's boy who, from being the lucky recipient of a 25-shilling windfall, rose to become 'The richest Burgess in the Civic Annals of the City of Durham'.

So, no bells and no pantomime cat but how, one wonders, would John Duck's fortunes have fared, if not for a careless corvid, a harassed herdsman and a golden coin?

The Rookhope Ryde

In the 18th and 19th centuries, Rookhope, in Weardale, was a grimy, bustling centre for the smelting of lead ore, mined from the surrounding moors. For centuries before that, however, the route through the Rookhope Valley, linking the fertile lands along the River Wear in the south with Allendale, Northumberland and the lawless border regions in the north, had been frequented by all kinds of wayfarers and travellers; some of these had been welcome, some had not.

Border Reivers, Steel Bonnets, Mosstroopers, are some of the names given today to the lawless border families and clans who made their living by raiding, thieving and cattle rustling across northern England and southern Scotland. These were wild, remote lands where the only laws heeded were those that these families had themselves decreed. They had loyalties neither to monarch nor to religion and they raided with impunity. The English stole from the Scottish and the Scots from the English, across a fluid, ill-defined and totally un-policed border. But there were also those Northumbrian clans, 'Masterful, dare-devil, desperadoes all', who were not averse to stealing from their cousins to the south.

In the year 1569 Charles Neville, the 6th Earl of Westmorland, sitting in the great baron's hall of his magnificent medieval fortress of Raby Castle, held council with a great array of northern nobles. They had taken the momentous decision to overthrow the Protestant Queen Elizabeth I and install the Catholic Mary, Queen of Scots as the new English monarch. Clearly, this was a very risky exercise, for failure would mean banishment, disinheritance or death. But the northern nobles were confident of their cause and, with the firm conviction that the ordinary Catholic people of England would rise up and follow them, in November 1569 they rode out of Brancepeth Castle with Charles Neville and Thomas Percy, the 7th Earl of Northumberland, at their head and made for Durham City – the 'Rising of the North' had begun. Soon afterwards the rebels advanced on Barnard Castle, where Sir George Bowes commanded forces loyal to Queen Elizabeth. A ten-day siege ensued and the fate of the 'Rising' hung in the balance.

Of course, the actions of the Earl of Westmorland and his County Durham retainers had not gone unnoticed by those, perhaps with less grand ambitions, who lived a little further north. And so it was that they quickly drew up their own plans:

For Weardale men is a journey taen,
They are so far out o'er yon fell,
That some of them's with the two Earls,
And others fast in Bernard Castell.

They reasoned that with Weardale largely emptied of the earl's retainers, there would be rich and undefended pickings to be had along the Wear Valley. A force of Tynedale mosstroopers, therefore, made up from men from Thirlwall in Northumberland and from Willeva, described by 19th-century chroniclers as a small district or township in the parish of Lanercost, made their way down, to help themselves to whatever they could carry or drive away. The story of the ensuing raid was recorded in verse form just three years after the actual event and down the following centuries, it was often recited as oral tradition.

On 6th December 1569, barely a month after the noble rebels had marched under their banners out of Brancepeth, a band of mosstroopers under the banners of their own leaders, Harry Corbyl, Simon Fell and Martin Ridley, set off from their Northumberland strongholds early in the morning, to take plunder in Weardale. Before noon they rested on the moors above Rookhope. They were in confident mood. Surely only women, the old and the young would be left to protect valuable livestock and anything else worth taking from the rich lands along the banks of the River Wear. Down from the head of the Rookhope Valley they came, as far on as Wolsingham, so some said, and in four hours had stealthily rounded up more than six hundred sheep, horses and cattle. Content with their plunder, they began their slow journey back up the Rookhope Valley, to the north, and safety. What they didn't know, however, was that they had been watched and hasty arrangements were being made to intercept them.

Their progress had first been witnessed by a Weardale man, Rowland Emerson, and, upon his word, the alarm had been raised and had spread like wildfire all along the valley. News of the raid came to the bailiff's house at Eastgate. The bailiff was not at home but his wife, knowing where he could be found, quickly sent a messenger to him with his horse, his jacket of mail and his weapons: all that he would need to confront the robbers. When the messenger reached him, it is said that a mixture of both fear and anger swelled in his soul, for it had been only three days before that his own brother had been terribly injured by border thieves who had inflicted upon him 'nineteen bloody wounds'.

A band of about fifty men and boys, mostly farm workers, was hastily assembled. With hardly any experience of fighting against an armed and dangerous foe, they set off to pursue the raiders up the five miles of the Rookhope Valley and take back, at whatever cost, what was theirs.

The Tynedale men were twice that number and they had a head start. They couldn't travel quickly, however, hampered as they were by the stolen beasts they drove. But they were not concerned. They thought that their ferocious and merciless reputation preceded them and they believed that there was none left in Weardale who would dare to challenge them. But challenged they were: 'For he that bears his head so high, he oft times falls into the dyke.' The Weardale men overtook the robbers at Neukton Cleugh, near the head of the Rookhope Valley, and blocked their way north. But the mosstroopers were not some as would simply flee, for they 'Feared neither Heaven nor Hell'. Battle lines, of sorts, were ordered and a ferocious fight ensued.

It lasted more than an hour and when it was over four Tynedale men lay dead, many were wounded and eleven taken prisoner. Of the Weardale men, only one perished, the same man who had first raised the alarm, Rowland Emerson. The victorious men from Weardale took back what was theirs. For the mosstroopers, the Rookhope Ryde, or Rookhope Raid, had failed and the humbled Tynedale robbers limped their bloodied and bruised way back up the northern road.

The 'Rising of the North' also failed; the rebels were utterly defeated. Thomas Percy, Earl of Northumberland died on the scaffold. Charles Neville, Earl of Westmorland escaped into an exile from which he would never return and his entire estates were forfeited to Queen Elizabeth. Retribution was merciless. Sixty-six rebels were executed in Durham City alone and it was the claim of the loyal Sir George Bowes that in an area of the country '60 miles in length and 20 in breadth, between Newcastle and Wetherby, there was hardly a town or village where he had not executed at least one of the inhabitants.'

All this was as may be but it was not the 'Rising of the North' that was recorded in verse, at least not by the people of Weardale. The significance of the fall of two of the mightiest and most ancient families in Northern England was as nothing to the brave repelling of a band of a hundred Tynedale mosstroopers that day in December 1569, by a few ordinary Weardale men:

> *Lord, send us peace, into the realm,*
> *That every man may live on his own!*
> *I trust to God, if it be his will,*
> *That Weardale men may never be overthrown.*

Nail Your Colours
to the Mast

It was just a normal Sunday in October; the parishioners in attendance at St John's church, Sunderland were paying pious and patient attention to the words of the rector, with the organist, Mr Haswell, filling the church with solemn music. Suddenly the north door clattered open and a breathless man was seemingly blown inside by the east coast wind. As the rector and the startled congregation turned to see what trouble had arrived and to hear whatever pronouncement the man had to make, they were loudly informed: 'Admiral Duncan's defeated the Dutch fleet at Camperdown!'

Mr Haswell turned to his keyboard and immediately struck up a loud and stirring version of *Rule Britannia* and the congregation as one, without the bidding of the rector, responded by singing the refrain. For the British Navy had indeed won another hard-fought victory on the high seas; but for the moment, those Sunderland churchgoers could not have known the significance the victory would have for one, until then obscure, individual of their seagoing fraternity.

Britain has a long and proud tradition of seafaring and, of course, of famous naval victories, crucial at times for the survival of the nation: Nelson's defeat of the French fleet at Trafalgar, the dispersal and sinking of the Spanish Armada, even back to distant Anglo-Saxon days and the wooden warships deployed by King Alfred the Great against the Danish Viking invaders of his day. But perhaps a victory less well known to the general British public is the victory of a British fleet under the command of Admiral Duncan, the Royal Navy's Commander in Chief of the North Seas, against the Dutch, in October 1797.

Britain was on high alert. Napoleon Bonaparte was sweeping all Europe before him and he was attempting to bring together all the ships captured from the defeated Spanish and Dutch fleets to support an invasion of England. It was imperative for Britain that he was not allowed to do so. The 19th-century chronicler M.A. Richardson tells us in his *Table Book* that: 'The aspect of affairs at this period was peculiarly alarming, especially in maritime districts, where the utmost exertions were deemed necessary to meet impending invasion. Whilst our ports were infested with Press Gangs, and our coasts covered with military camps ... with the French daily expected to land.'

Once again British ships stood between their homeland and a foreign aggressor, their orders being to sink or take as a prize all enemy vessels. With a fleet of around eighteen ships, Admiral Duncan had been blockading a Dutch force of about the same strength but on 11th October, the Dutch made a move to break out. Duncan immediately gave the order to his captains to attack. The two forces opened fire on each other in shallow coastal waters not far from the Dutch village of Camperdown.

The fighting was fierce as Duncan's flagship, the *Venerable*, letting fly her seventy-four guns, made straight for the Dutch flagship, the *Vryheid*. But the first attack was unsuccessful and the situation quickly worsened when three more Dutch ships turned their guns as one on the *Venerable*. Things were looking bleak as shot, shell and splinters caused bloody carnage on the British flagship. As always, the rallying points for both fleets were the colours on display on their flagship; as long as the colours flew, the battle was not lost and fighting men were spurred on to further fury.

In a statement worthy of Nelson himself, Admiral Duncan had said to one of his captains just before engaging the enemy fleet, 'I have taken the depth of the water, and when the *Venerable* goes down, my flag will still fly.' But time and time again during the battle, the mast of the *Venerable* was hit, until eventually, shattered and splintered, it broke asunder and the British colours came tumbling down. If the rest of the fleet were to see this, they would assume defeat and surrender; they might stop fighting, and whatever they did they must keep on fighting.

So it was that a 22-year-old seaman picked up the colours from the blood-stained deck, climbed up through smashed and rent rigging, all the time being exposed to shot, shrapnel and splinter, until, when he had climbed as high as he could, he nailed the British colours to what was left of the mast. The flag flew and the British fleet rallied. In the nick of time another British vessel, the *Triumph*, came to the assistance of the *Venerable* and both ships now fired devastating broadsides into the Dutch flagship, bringing down her masts. Shortly afterwards, the Dutch commander, Admiral De Winter, lowered his own colours in sign of surrender, his flagship now little more than an 'unmanageable hulk'.

The human cost of the battle was terrible, with the British losing a hundred and ninety-one dead, with a further five hundred and sixty wounded. It was reported that the Dutch losses were around twice that. Eleven Dutch ships were taken as prizes. They would no longer pose a threat to English shores.

To Admiral Duncan went the glory, or at least most of it. He was created a peer, Viscount Duncan of Camperdown, and granted a pension of £2,000 a year, both for himself and for his two succeeding heirs. The Freedom of the City of London was also his and he was presented with a sword valued at two hundred guineas. Special gold medals were even struck in honour of his victory. But what of the heroic seaman who had risked his life to nail his colours to the mast, and by doing so had rallied the British fleet to ultimate victory?

His name was Jack (John) Crawford, and he had been born in Pottery Bank in Sunderland. The son of a keelman on the River Wear he had, from childhood, been at home on the sea and as a youth he had served an apprenticeship aboard a vessel out of South Shields. It is not known for certain how Jack ended up in the Navy; some reports, possibly with an eye for the romantic or probably just more sympathetic to the 'Senior Service', told that it had been in response to a family argument that he had run away and joined up, to pursue a life at sea. The obvious alternative is, of course, that he, like many other men from coastal towns, had been very unromantically 'pressed' into service. But however it came about, Jack Crawford survived his heroics at the Battle of Camperdown, although he was shot through the cheek during his climb, which necessitated him being fed through a straw for some weeks after.

The following year the citizens of Sunderland presented Jack with a specially-struck silver medal, engraved, 'The town of Sunderland to John Crawford, for gallant services, the 11th October, 1797'. Indeed he received many other symbols of recognition, both locally and nationally. It is said that he walked, wearing his Camperdown medal on his chest, in procession to St Paul's Cathedral behind the funeral cortège of Admiral Lord Nelson. He was even presented to King George III and it is reported that when the monarch asked if he were to offer a royal reward for the heroics of John Crawford, what would

the young man choose, Jack, the son of a Sunderland keelman, replied simply, 'A new keel.'

Eventually, Jack left the Navy with a pension of thirty pounds a year and did indeed return to being a keelman. It is said that he was made an offer of a hundred pounds a week, then a phenomenal sum of money to someone like him, to act out on stage a nightly reconstruction of his 'Nailing the Colours to the Mast' at the Battle of Camperdown. But he wouldn't, saying, 'No, I will never disgrace the real act of a sailor by acting like a play fool.' But, unfortunately, Jack did like a drink and he was no good with money. Therefore, he was constantly in debt. He even had to pawn his Camperdown medal. It would be twenty-nine years before it was redeemed.

In 1808 he married and lived out the rest of his life as a family man, until cholera descended upon Sunderland in 1831. Jack was poor and lived in a poor area of the town, an area 'calculated to invite the pestilence'. He soon contracted the disease and died on 10th November of that year, aged just fifty-six, the second victim of the outbreak.

After his death and burial in an unmarked grave, an attempt was made to establish, at the public's expense, a permanent memorial to Sunderland's own 'Hero of Camperdown'. Benefit evenings were held to raise money but nothing came of it and it was not until 1887, when a report of his exploits of ninety years earlier was published in the *Monthly Chronicle*, that interest in him was once again aroused.

There were detractors, as there always are, and those who would do down a reputation. A century after the event, a 'local historian' claimed that he was in possession of accounts from 'reliable witnesses', stating that Crawford, when carrying out his famous action, had been 'drunk, acting without orders, and should have been Court Martialled'. The fact that he was witnessed by the commander of the *Triumph*, in the very action for which he later had been lauded, seemed no longer to matter.

The sexton and bellringer of Holy Trinity church, Sunderland, old John Crosby, had, after Jack's original burial in an unmarked grave, planted a tree over him and recorded where that tree grew. At that same spot, on Monday, 6th August 1888, a ceremony took place to unveil a permanent headstone. The headstone, paid for by public subscription and draped with the very flag that Jack had nailed to the mast of the *Venerable*, was unveiled by the then Earl of Camperdown, the grandson of Admiral Duncan. Finally, Jack Crawford would have a marker befitting his memory, although the unsympathetic 'local historian', denounced it as a 'Deplorable Monument'. A permanent public memorial was also commissioned – a heroic bronze statue depicting Jack in the very action of 'Nailing his Colours to the Mast'. It was unveiled by the Earl of Camperdown two years later, in Mowbray Park, in Sunderland.

And so it is that today, over 200 years after his heroic actions, he can still be seen there, frozen for all time in his moment of glory: Jack Crawford – the Hero of Camperdown!

A Ransom for a Bishop

~

You may or may not have heard the saying that there are those individuals of perhaps questionable ability, across all professions, who are 'Promoted to their level of Incompetence'. This may well have been said, though no doubt not to his face, of the 14th-century Prince Bishop of Durham, Lewis de Beaumont.

The Durham monks had strenuously opposed Beaumont's election, arguing that he lacked the requisite learning. In fact they'd even elected someone of their own choosing, Henry de Stamford, Prior of Finchale. To make matters worse, the King's choice was someone else completely, Thomas Carleton, his Keeper of the Privy Seal. But Beaumont was of noble birth and, as well as being Treasurer of Salisbury Cathedral, he was also a cousin of Queen Isabella, affectionately known as the 'She Wolf of France'. Isabella persuaded the King against Carleton, his own choice, and pushed for the election of her kinsman. She was also supported by the most powerful nobles, who threatened that 'should a monk be elected, they would cut off his head'.

So it was that Beaumont was called to the See of Durham. He was now very powerful, and he was already very rich; but he was a 'foreigner' with little or no knowledge of, or interest in, the County Palatine of Durham. And apparently, so the monkish chroniclers tell, he was not appropriately educated for his new station. He didn't understand Latin, having to take lessons before his investiture when, to the horror of those around him, he made a mess of his solemn vows. But a new Prince Bishop, especially one with royal connections, descending in all his pomp and splendour upon Durham, was a tempting prize for one of the most notorious of the north's robber barons, Sir Gilbert de Middleton.

County Durham in the early 14th century was a lawless place.

Following the English defeat at the Battle of Bannockburn, the Scots made frequent raids into the county, terrifying the inhabitants with fire and slaughter. The weak English king, Edward II, seemed unable, or unwilling, to change that situation. As a result, many of the county's knights and barons had simply taken matters into their own hands, and began to subject the people to their own laws.

King Edward, in his desire for peace with Scotland, had petitioned the Pope for emissaries to assist in his negotiations with the Scots, and two cardinals had been sent from Rome, Gaucelin Deuze and Luca di Fieschi. Their mission was to deliver Papal Letters to Robert the Bruce so they rode north with Lewis de Beaumont and his brother, Henry, then the Constable of the Prince Bishop's castle at Norham on Tweed, with the intention of being in attendance at Beaumont's investiture in Durham Cathedral.

In August 1317 the party left London for Scotland and reached Darlington on the 31st, where the new Bishop and the Papal representatives slept, before resuming their journey to Durham. However, it was at Darlington that a messenger arrived and warned them that they were likely to be waylaid on the road, should they journey further north. But the new Bishop, claiming that the Scots King would not dare attempt such a thing, but probably also thinking that it was merely a ploy by the Durham monks, to delay or dissuade him from entering Durham, dismissed the warning and again, with his great retinue following, stepped out onto the Great North Road and cast his covetous eyes towards St Cuthbert's city.

The journey of 1st September was initially uneventful and the Bishop no doubt thought to himself how wise he had been to ignore the obviously insincere warning. At length, they came to a place called Rushyford, just south of Ferryhill and described then as being an area of stagnant pools and a small rivulet, surrounded by boggy ground. This, the party had to carefully pick their way through, and following its successful negotiation, they cast their eyes back onto the road. They were at once surrounded by a large force of mounted and heavily-armed men. These were mostly northern landowners, who 'all driven to desperation by their misfortunes', had become 'shavaldores', a term used to describe 'Gentleman Brigands of the Scottish Borders', but their number also included Northumbrians and Yorkshiremen. They were led by Sir Gilbert de Middleton and they did not look as if they had come to pay their respects to the new Bishop and his party. Soon enough, their intentions were made clear.

The Bishop elect and his brother were taken and carried away as hostages to Mitford Castle in Northumberland. At first the cardinals were left alone, but it seems that Middleton lost control over some of his men, who proceeded to relieve the Papal Emissaries of their valuables. To win back some favour, Middleton apologised, gave them a horse each and guaranteed their safe passage to Durham City. But failing to prevent the attack on the churchmen had been Middleton's fatal mistake, 'nothing would satisfy the Cardinals themselves but his cruel punishment.'

After being insulted by Middleton, the cardinals made their way to Durham, where they arrived with just the horses they had been given and the clothes they wore. But it was a state of affairs from which they still managed to profit. They sent their Papal Letters on to Scotland by messenger and, before returning to York, they ensured that they were richly compensated by the monks of Durham for their dreadful and humiliating ordeal, with new clothes, bedding and comforts, new horses, sacred vestments and, in the case of Luca di Fieschi, a pension of a hundred florins for the rest of his life. And it is also said that before they even left for York, Middleton met with the cardinals at Durham, restoring to them much of what had been taken, to try and make amends for what he realised had been a major mistake and to ask for their absolution – 'but in this he gained very little'. On reaching York they immediately published a death sentence on Middleton and his followers.

In supporting the Prior of Finchale as their own candidate for bishop, the monks of Durham had demonstrated that they didn't want Beaumont, who, as they had already made quite clear, they didn't like. So it must have been particularly galling when the King ordered them to pay Beaumont's ransom, 'a great and intolerable sum of money', necessitating, we are told, having to sell off some of their treasures to raise the cash. But this they did and he was duly released. However, if they believed that this would put them in a more favourable light with their new Bishop, then their belief was sadly misplaced. For on his return, Beaumont pronounced, 'Do nothing for me, as I will do nothing for you; pray for my death, for whilst I live, you will get nothing from me.' Clearly, future relationships between monks and Bishop were going to be challenging.

Eventually, Mitford Castle, stronghold of the kidnapper and robber baron, was stormed and overrun and, 'rushing with blows upon him', Middleton himself was taken prisoner, bound in chains and hauled off, eventually to stand before the King in London, where he arrived on 21st January 1318, with his feet tied beneath his horse. He was put in the Tower, before being brought in front of the King at Westminster five days later. And if he was hoping for the grant of mercy from a weak king, he was sadly mistaken.

Accused of treason, promotion of war within the kingdom of England, sedition, theft, kidnap and extortion, his fate was well and truly sealed. Edward ordered that Middleton be dragged through the city to the gallows, there to be hanged, his body torn open before being beheaded. His heart and organs were to be burnt at the gallows and his head spiked on a pole in London. His body was then to be divided into four parts, to be sent and nailed to the city walls at Newcastle, York, Bristol and Dover. It is said that to ensure satisfaction and to witness justice being done, the two cardinals were present at the execution.

As for Lewis de Beaumont, the church histories tell us that the rest of his career as Bishop of Durham was used mainly to build up fortunes for himself and his relatives. Clearly, relations between him and the monks remained strained, with the monkish historian Robert de Graystanes describing him as: 'Avaricious, not caring how he got money, and spending it improvidently on an enormous household. He was not a priest, not having been educated as a priest.'

Yet there is a curious irony in this. After his death Beaumont was buried in a place of great honour, in front of the High Altar of Durham Cathedral. Had the monks of Durham eventually changed their opinion of him? Perhaps there was more to the career of Lewis de Beaumont than has been recorded in the histories written by those who never wanted him in the first place.

Lang Man; Tall Tale

County Durham is well served with legendary creatures: monstrous worms, savage giant boars and denizens of the Fairy Realm, both benevolent and sinister. There have been written down and recorded over the county's long history many strange tales of disparate ghosts, boggles, sprites and hags, and, of course, tales of giants. But perhaps one of the most atmospheric and elusive tales of the county, is that of the *Lang Man o' Bollyhope.*

The story goes that long ago two mysterious figures did battle on the edge of Bollihope Fell in Weardale. The reason? Well, that is not really known, but it is said that the scene of the fateful conflict was on top of a high ridge, overlooking the valley of the River Wear, near Wolsingham.

It seems that, as with many such stories, one version is never sufficient. And true to form, different interpretations of the Lang Man have been handed down over the years. It is for the reader to choose which, if any, is their favourite.

One version, which can quickly be dismissed as true legend, is that the two combatants were indeed giants, quarrelling over their Weardale hunting grounds. Inevitably, the quarrel developed into violence and eventually one of the giants was laid low under the furious blows of the other's club.

A second version, perhaps more plausible, at least for those disposed to the romantic, was related in verse by Richard Watson, 'the Teesdale Poet', when, in 1884, his long poem entitled *The Long Man of Bollihope Fell* was printed:

> *Such were the scenes of closing day,*
> *As two men slowly took their way,*
> *Where Bollihope's limpid waters glide,*
> *And climbed the dark brown mountain side …*

Watson not only tells of two human combatants – a young man and another, a very tall and fearsome individual – but also gives their identities and a motive for their life and death struggle. For he tells in his lines that the drama acted out was the revenge of a brother for his young sister, who had been beguiled by the very tall man, who had a very dark character, and taken by him far from the family home, only for her to suffer miserably at his hands and eventually die a sad death, from neglect and the want of true love.

Eventually, the grieving brother caught up with the one responsible for his sister's death. And the challenge was made:

> *Here we meet in mortal strife,*
> *Draw your sword, defend thy life!*

And so their destiny was set and they began the struggle that was witnessed by those in the valley, far below:

> *Then hand to hand they both engaged,*
> *And long and fierce the combat raged.*

Eventually, after much fighting, and many verses, the young man had his revenge and brought his giant opponent crashing to the ground. His quest achieved, he simply walked away from the scene of his victory, never to be seen again. His victim it was who was buried the next day in the grave of the Lang Man.

However, if we reclaim the story from the mythical world of legendary giants or indeed from the romantic world of Victorian poets, we are left with a simple tale. The story, as related in the mid 19th century by the chronicler Maurice Denham, is quite brief and simply told.

Late one fine evening, two figures were seen high up on the fell by the residents of the valley bottom. The mysterious figures 'at once proceeded to mortal strife'. The people watched as the combatants fought on, long and hard, their forms picked out by the slanting rays of the lowering sun and silhouetted against the clear blue evening sky:

> *The Warriors on the mountain high,*
> *moving athwart the evening sky,*
> *seem'd forms of Giant height!*
> *Their armour as it caught the rays,*
> *flash'd back again the western blaze,*
> *in lines of dazzling light.*

61

But this was clearly a fight to the death, there had to be a victor and a vanquished and, at length, one of the figures did indeed fall. The other, standing victorious as his opponent's life faded with the last rays of the sun, waited and watched until he had final assurance of his victory, then he melted away with the evening light.

The next morning the people from the valley, emboldened by the morning sunlight, made their way, as Denham described it, '*up a dreary and sterile track*' to the scene of the drama. There they found the pitifully mangled corpse of a tall man. Nobody knew him, and nobody afterwards asked after him. So this tall mysterious warrior was buried where he fell and a cairn of stones was raised over his body. But, of course, questions unanswered by facts lend themselves to legendary solutions.

So it was that the two unknown combatants witnessed that fair evening became transmogrified into legendary beings from another realm, their exploits, and their story, gaining superhuman proportions. So much so, it was recorded that the clash of their weapons could be heard in the valley bottom, as their human forms were dilated into the stature of the giants of old. The 19th-century Durham historian William Fordyce relates another even more colourful tradition, which tells that the '*Awe-Stricken*' spectators had witnessed the mortal combat against the beautiful but, to them, fearful backdrop of a display of the *aurora borealis*.

So the story of the two giants, or the two warriors, or the vengeful brother and his callous foe, has been told in prose and in verse, and is today firmly established in the world of County Durham legend. And yet the actual grave of the *Lang Man o' Bollyhope* can still be seen, high up on the same Weardale ridge. A cairn of stones, or, as Denham described it, a '*currock*' obviously of superhuman proportions lies today over his resting place, and a solitary marker stone is set at one end for his remembrance.

> *And shepherds still the legend tell,*
> *Of the 'Long Man of Bollihope Fell'!*

And as for the story of the mortal combat that took place on that very spot so long ago, well of course it may be true!

The Fate of Johnny's Money

This story takes place in the middle of the 18th century. It was the celebration of the half-yearly Rent Dinner for County Durham landowner Sir Ralph Millbanke, and surrounded by his retainers and tenant farmers the tables groaned under the weight of his hospitality.

A toast was raised to the health of the good landowner; it was the usual one, a little bit odd perhaps, but at least predictably so. And a predictably odd speech suited well the speech maker, one of Sir Ralph's chief tenants. His name was Johnny Wardell, sometimes recorded as Weardale, which may give an indication as to the origins of his antecedents.

'I'll gie ye a worthy and respectable gentleman, Mr. Ralph Millbanke, esquire, Knight and Baron-Knight. I'm certain sure ye'll all drink it heartily, with all the honours, as we're all in duty bound. Lang may he live, and be a blessing to ivery yin connected wi' 'im, and when he's called upon at length to his last account, may he get a full quittance for ony mistyeaks he may have made, and get a front seat i' heevin.'

Johnny Wardell was Sir Ralph Millbanke's tenant farmer at Ketton, at that time described as being in the township of Brafferton, about two miles from Aycliffe. He was known to be an odd man and, judging by his appearance alone, seemed to be a poor one; however, as we know, appearances can be deceptive.

But Johnny dutifully farmed his land and, when the occasion arose, took his produce to market. His usual haunts were Barnard Castle and Darlington but Darlington Market only traded livestock, so when he had corn to sell, Johnny had to wander abroad, crossing the River Tees into Yorkshire to attend the market at Richmond. He always left the night before to enable him to arrive in time for the opening of business, and to ensure that no potential sale was lost.

To save himself money he would transport his own corn, with the assistance only of his 'lad'. A string of six or eight pack horses would be employed, each carrying a couple of sacks of grain, and in this fashion he would set off, with himself on the lead horse, seated on a cheap, home-made 'sods and sunks' saddle, made of sackcloth stuffed with straw, and the other horses roped together, with his lad riding on the hindmost, bringing up the rear.

When their destination had been reached, Johnny would unload his corn at the market and then his lad would take the horses back out of the town, to a place previously agreed, there to await Johnny's return, after completion of his business. In this way Johnny avoided paying any fees for the stabling and feeding of his steeds. Provender for the two men would be carried with them, the usual victuals consisting of Johnny's home-made rye bread, spread with thin, home-made cheese, all washed down with water. And, unsurprisingly perhaps, it was said that there was no shopkeeper or stabler, innkeeper or ostler in either town that 'ever saw a penny of Johnny's money'.

But it was not just because of his parsimonious habits that Johnny was a well-known figure. His regular outfit was of a singular style. He normally wore a homespun grey coat, made from the wool of his own sheep, which had been spun by his wife and daughters; and to this end, apart from the hard grind of daily work on the farm, the whole of their leisure time was taken up with this occupation. His feet were shod with rough hobnailed shoes and to cover his legs to above his knees, he wore coarse woollen stockings, or 'hoggers'. To crown his strange costume, Johnny wore breeches made of well-tanned sheep hide. Nothing particularly strange there, the reader might think, but these breeches were in fact a curious form of family heirloom, for they had also been worn by both his father and his grandfather. Aged as they were, however, they did serve more than their one obvious purpose. It was said that, as if to recognise and celebrate their accumulated years, the breeches had attracted such a thick layer of grease and dirt that, with the aid of an old nail, they served as a latter-day Roman wax tablet for the totting up of Johnny's market accounts.

And it was in this singular attire that Johnny turned up one day to the auction of a valuable property; a property that he was seriously interested in buying. This was a farm, situated on the road to Croft, and it went by the curious name of Stickabitch. Johnny made plain his intentions, but he had serious competition. Many of the local gentry were there, together with a number of moneyed and influential individuals from Darlington and Durham City, all looking for whatever bargains there were to be had.

Those selling the farm looked dubiously at Johnny, seriously doubting that this vision of relentless thrift that now stood before them could possibly have the inclination, or the money, to see the auction through to an actual purchase. And the assembled gentry eyed Johnny with suspicion and contempt as they huffed, puffed and muttered to themselves, their faces flushing under their big wigs; and they were all outbid by Johnny Wardell.

For his part, Johnny assured the vendors that he did indeed have the money to cover the purchase and he proceeded to produce, from the hidden recesses of his curious outfit, an old stocking. And from the old stocking he proceeded to empty a large number of almost new golden guineas – golden guineas that bore on one side the image of King Charles II, who had died well over half a century before. So it was that, much to the astonishment of all present, all that is apart from himself, Johnny Wardell got his Stickabitch Farm, paying the whole price of the property there and then and insisting that the deeds be handed over to him without delay.

Johnny, who had long since acquired the, perhaps not proud, but certainly appropriate sobriquet of the 'Miser of Ketton', once told an individual who had the temerity to suggest to him that with his mean habits he was simply storing up money, only for it to be spent by his children, 'Bairns, lads! If they have as much pleasure in spending it as I have in gathering it, then let them be doing it.'

But this generosity of spirit did not extend to his neighbour, Mr Stephenson of Brafferton, whom, partial as he was to the latest fashion and to expensive follies, Johnny considered to be a fool and a spendthrift. When Stephenson splashed out on a pack of hounds, Johnny, on witnessing them tearing across their owner's land, predicted to his sons that the cost of their upkeep would have to be offset by the unnecessary sale of good timber from Stephenson's estate. Sure enough, Johnny's prediction came true, and when Stephenson subsequently bought another, more expensive pack of hunting dogs, Johnny was heard to say after catching their braying on the wind, 'Lads, de ye but hear 'em? They're roarin out land and all; land and all.' And he was right again, as in a short time the follies of Mr Stephenson had cost him 'a complete havoc of timber, land; and all he had'.

But Johnny was quite happy, thank you very much, with what he had, and not just in his earthly life. Once, when questioned about his hopes for eternity, he replied: 'They may talk of Heaven as they will; but give me Ketton Greens.' Of course, this was a very apposite remark for the speaker, for Ketton Greens was a particularly fertile tract of land which, it is recorded, grew seven crops of oats in seven years and made Johnny a lot of money. Indeed, Johnny the Miser ended his days owning a substantial amount of valuable property and land, including, so the chronicles tell, High Beaumont Hill, Aycliffe Wood, Chapel House opposite Gainford, and, of course, Stickabitch Farm.

There is a saying, probably French, which states that 'Gaming is the offspring of avarice'. There is another saying, no doubt English, which states that 'Gear hardly won, is lightly spent'. In Johnny Wardell's case, both were to prove appropriate and prophetic. For Johnny's grandsons were said to have been 'great men at bets', who, we are told, associated with that other great man of bets – the Prince Regent, later King George IV. And they were certainly true to the words of the 'Miser of Ketton'. For, with the wealth that Johnny had relentlessly accumulated over years of parsimonious living, they did indeed have as much pleasure in spending it as he'd had in gathering it. To such an extent, so the chronicles tell, that 'They spirited Johnny's estates through the air.'

The Conqueror and the Saint

Durham Cathedral was built to house the body of St Cuthbert of Lindisfarne. Since AD 995 many pilgrims have visited his resting place: kings and commoners, the mighty and the humble have all made their way through the narrow streets of the old city, to seek his blessings and make their offerings.

In the year 1027 Cnut the Great, Viking emperor, King of England, Denmark and Norway, the King Canute of watery legend, sometime after failing to hold back the tide, walked six miles to the city, barefoot, head shaven and dressed as a penitent, to prostrate himself before the saint and bestow gifts of riches and land upon his monkish guardians. However, not all royal visitors were so generous or so respectful. Forty-five years after Cnut, another foreign conqueror, William, Duke of Normandy, also paid a visit to the saint, with consequences which that mighty king could not possibly have foreseen.

Cuthbert was born around AD 634 in the Lammermuir Hills, in what is today lowland Scotland. After seeing a vision of the soul of St Aidan of Lindisfarne ascending to Heaven, he joined the abbey at Melrose in AD 651 and began a life in holy orders. He travelled extensively across the wild and turbulent lands of Northumbria, where Paganism still thrived, where the spirits of wood and water were still worshipped and where the peasantry paid homage at sacred trees and wells. Against this background Cuthbert's reputation grew; whispers of miracles following his teachings spread amongst the populace, and he became the best loved of all the northern holy men. He became Prior of Lindisfarne in AD 665 but eleven years later he retreated, seeking the solitude of Inner Farne, off the Northumberland coast, within sight of the Northumbrian royal stronghold of Bamburgh Castle. After nine years as a recluse, on Easter Day AD 685, he was elected Bishop of Lindisfarne and was widely regarded as a living saint. After only two more years, on 20th March AD 687, he died. His body was returned to Lindisfarne for burial and a shrine erected over his resting place. Soon, more stories began to circulate about miracles happening at his tomb, whispered reports from visiting pilgrims. His reputation, not just as a holy man but as 'The Wonder Worker of England' was being enhanced in death.

It was the custom of the time to open the coffin of a man of great sanctity between ten and twenty years after burial, the purpose being to wash the bones and wrap them in precious silks for ceremonial reburial. No doubt at least half an eye would also have been kept on the healthy, and lucrative, trade in holy relics. In AD 698, Cuthbert's coffin was duly opened and with that his saintliness, if any had doubted it, was proved. He appeared lying on his side, as if sleeping peacefully; after eleven years there was no sign of corruption on the body. It is thought that the monk Eadmer produced the precious Lindisfarne Gospels in reaction to this singular event. The 'Cult' of Cuthbert was now firmly established; his name, already renowned throughout the north, began to attract large numbers of pilgrims and visitors bearing gifts.

However, visitors of a more unwelcome kind arrived in June AD 793, when Norwegian raiders landed on the island and sacked the monastery. The *Anglo-Saxon Chronicles* tell us: 'The ravages of heathen men miserably destroyed God's church on Lindisfarne, with plunder and slaughter.' Those monks that were not killed were taken into slavery. The Viking Age in Britain had begun. The raiders took riches, offerings, anything they could carry, but the most precious possessions of the monastery, the incorrupt body of the saint and the illuminated gospels, written in his honour, were overlooked by the Norsemen.

Within a hundred years, however, the Viking threat had returned, when 'The Great Heathen Army' of Halfdan Wide Embrace and Ivar the Boneless, the sons of Ragnar Lodbrock, landed in England. So it was that in AD 875, the monks of Lindisfarne, fearing for their lives and for their holy relics, left the island, at the height of King Alfred the Great's war against the Danes, taking with them the body of their saint and their gospels, and began an epic journey across the North Country. It was a journey that would lead them eventually, in the year AD 995, to the Dun-Holme, a high rocky peninsula, covered in woodland and almost totally surrounded by a river, where a little church of branches and boughs became the prototype of the great cathedral that stands at Durham today.

William, Duke of Normandy invaded Anglo-Saxon England in October 1066, and following his victory at the Battle of Hastings, gradually swept all before him, ruthlessly putting down resistance to his rule. In 1072 he pushed on to the Scottish border, to receive the submission of their King, Malcolm. On his return, he stopped at his garrison at Durham, gave the order to begin the construction of a castle and decided to make Durham the centre of administrative and military affairs in the far north of his kingdom. William had come from overseas at the head of an army bent on conquest and with a few thousand knights and freebooters had seized a country with a population of over a million. The Conqueror was now all powerful and the time had come when he would challenge the sanctity of St Cuthbert himself.

The stories of the great northern saint and of the incorrupt state of his body had reached his ear but he did not believe them. He insisted on inspecting the body of the saint himself. The monks, perhaps understandably, argued against it and tried to persuade William not to do so. However, recognising as they did the temperament and the reputation of this particular king, the monkish chronicler Simeon of Durham relates that 'several Bishops and Abbots then present assented to his will, and thought it proper that the King's pleasure should be complied with.' However, as the clerics prevaricated, William grew suspicious and angry and he solemnly vowed that if he was deceived and the story of the incorrupt body of the saint was 'merely a tale to work upon the superstition of the vulgar', he would put to death 'all those of superior rank throughout the City who had presumed to impose on him'. The King commanded that the tomb be opened and the monks of Durham prayed for their deliverance.

The scene was set, it was All Saints' Day, 1072. Simeon relates that as the tomb was opened, William 'found himself smitten by a sudden burning fever, which distracted him in an intolerable manner'. Seized with terror at the thought of being struck down for his insolence by the wrath of the saint, the King rushed from the church, leaving untasted a great banquet that had been prepared in his honour. He instantly mounted his horse and sped from the city. Tradition has it that he fled down what is today Dun Cow Lane and out through a gate in the city wall, where Bow Lane now stands. Then on down to a ford in the river, he crossed and climbed the opposite bank 'never abating the speed of his horse till he arrived on the banks of the Tees', about thirty miles south of Durham. The gate in the wall

associated with the story became known as the King's Gate; Kingsgate Bridge, linking the peninsula with New Elvet, towers today over the scene of William's flight. The Conqueror had finally met his match. Of course, the story of the dread King's flight and the indication of God's displeasure at the attempt to disturb the sacred body overawed the people of Durham and no doubt contributed greatly to the veneration, and offerings, gifted to the saint's shrine.

Thirty-two years after the Conqueror's flight, the day came at last for the translation of the body of St Cuthbert into the great Norman cathedral that was still being built around him. On 24th August 1104 the coffin, in preparation for this sacred event, was ceremonially opened and the saint's body was found to be still incorrupt, the joints quite flexible and the air sweet smelling with the 'odour of sanctity'. For almost another 450 years the faithful made their way to Durham to seek the blessings of St Cuthbert, until, early in 1541, the hammer of the Reformation smashed down upon his shrine and eight and a half centuries of pilgrimage and devotion to him lay shattered and broken. The saint's body, 'whole, uncorrupt, and with his face bare and his beard, as it had been a fortnight's growth', was disinterred and his treasures, priceless relics of an epic story, were removed and scattered across the cathedral floor.

Thankfully, some are today in the care of Durham Cathedral and are on display as 'The Treasures of St Cuthbert'. However, the Lindisfarne Gospels, those magnificent illuminated manuscripts, written in honour of the saint, which had, for almost 550 years, been kept by his side at Durham, were taken and, to the continuing dismay and vexation of many, have been lost to Durham unto this day. The monks, those faithful guardians of St Cuthbert, took his body and reburied it under the simple marble slab that today bears his name – or did they?

But then, that perhaps is another story!

Hell's Kettles

The medieval mind often ascribed the dramatic and sometimes terrifying consequences of natural phenomena to the works of the Almighty and His Saints, or to the Devil and his Demons. The more dramatic and inexplicable the phenomenon, the more a supernatural explanation was clearly the correct one.

The year was 1179 and England was subject to the rule of the Plantagenet King Henry II. County Durham was subject to the episcopacy of Bishop Hugh of Le Puiset and it was on the Prince Bishop's land, just to the south of Darlington, that a singular and terrifying event took place: 'When the earth rose high at Oxenhale'.

The chronicler Roger of Howden, one of the King's secretaries, tells us simply that on Christmas Eve, as King Henry held his Court at Winchester, the people round about 'Oxenhale' witnessed the earth, to their horror, suddenly rising up like a dark tower, where it remained all day. Then, in the evening time, it came crashing back down with a terrible noise, 'to the terror of all who heard it'. Holes suddenly appeared in the earth and all the material that had, that very morning, been spewed out was now swallowed up. All that was left behind were deep pits, which proceeded to fill with angrily boiling water. From then on legends hung like shadows over these 'Kettles of Hell'.

Of course later, as with all good tales, the story was embellished and made even more sensational: 'In the land of Lord Hughe, Bishop of Duresme, the ground rose up to such a height that it was equal to the tops of the highest hills, and higher than the towers and spires of the churches.'

And the dark, sulphurous water, 'A hundred fathoms deep', that filled the cavities left behind, fumed and boiled like the 'Devil's Kettles'.

Indeed, it was a belief commonly held by local people, even up to the 16th century, that the pools were of diabolic origin. A belief confirmed, it seemed, by stories of passers-by telling that the lost souls of sinful men and women could sometimes be seen in their depths, their cries and yells heard in the surrounding fields. But as the centuries moved on and ages dawned that were perhaps more 'enlightened', a series of 'natural' or 'scientific' explanations for the phenomenon were put forward.

For example, they had probably been blown out by subterranean fires! This was a suggestion that no doubt did little to dissuade those who still held to a diabolic explanation. Or perhaps old collapsed coal workings, lime or alum pits were the cause. Many proposed an underground link with the nearby River Tees. This theory was apparently supported by a story that was told to the antiquarian chronicler of King Henry VIII, John Leland. The tale goes that a duck, which had been 'marked after the fashion of the Bishop of Durham', had been set free on one of the pools to dive and dabble at will. It was of no surprise to anyone that, some days later, the same duck, identifiable by its markings, was seen on the River Tees, near Croft Bridge. Confirmation indeed that the dabbling duck must have been sucked down into the watery pit, and by means of the subterranean passage had later been spewed out into the Tees. It has to be accepted, presumably, that the bird in question must have been flightless and, of course, the fact that when the water level in the River Tees rose and fell that of the 'Hell's Kettles' remained constant did little to dissuade those who remained convinced of the theory.

So it was that the story of the watery subterranean passage persisted. In later years in the telling and retelling of the tale, the duck was transmogrified into a goose and then, entering the realm of complete fiction, into a cow, which had apparently been grasped by the nose whilst drinking and dragged under the dark water by a giant pike, only to be seen some days later, floating in the Tees.

Such stories continued to be told and for over two hundred years the 'Hell's Kettles' continued to be a curiosity for the amazement of strangers – a '*must see*' on the itinerary of any visitor to the County Palatine. And, indeed, the pools did have some curious properties. Local people somehow discovered that the water from them curdled milk and it would not lather soap; but it was not until the 18th century that any sort of serious study was made of the 'Hell's Kettles'.

In 1774 a physical description of them was finally written down. There were four pools, it was said. Three of them were situated near to each other, the other some distance away, near the turnpike road. They were dutifully plumbed and, rather disappointingly, the bottomless pits were found to be no more than twenty feet deep. Of course, as is sometimes the case, when scientific investigation makes its entrance, superstition and legend tend to leave the stage.

A later story is told of an irreligious farmer, who, not heeding the sacred acknowledgements of a Saint's Day, proceeded across the fields hard by the pools, with his cart full of hay, on the Feast of St Barnabus, the 11th June. A neighbour reproached him for his disrespect, to which the farmer very poetically, but rather unwisely replied, 'Barnaby yea! Barnaby nay! I'll have my hay, whether God will; or nay.' Shortly afterwards, the farmer, his horses and his cartload of hay disappeared from the mortal world, swallowed up, it was said, by the deep waters of the 'Hell's Kettles'.

Of course, the phenomenon did have a natural explanation, an explanation in fact undoubtedly more concerned with hydrology and geomorphology, than with demonology. It is thought that the real culprit, far from being the sulphurs of Hell, was hydrated calcium sulphate, or gypsum. The process involved, I will now attempt to describe. However, I am certainly no geologist and if any reader is in full possession of the scientific certainties then I apologise unreservedly for the following, no doubt inadequate, explanation.

Gypsum, contained in the geological strata, was dissolved by fast-flowing subterranean water. When all was washed away, the earth above collapsed into the resulting cavity. The surrounding rock also collapsed in, sending rock, earth and debris shooting up and out through the newly-formed surface holes. Eventually, through gravity, all collapsed back and the flowing water filled up the resulting subterranean cavities. Over time the site has developed into an important natural habitat, which now supports a flora unusual for this part of the country. Indeed it has moved from being a place of terror to the medieval mind to a Site of Special Scientific Interest.

The Darlington historian W.H.D. Longstaffe, writing in 1854, attempted to put forward a natural explanation for the creation and survival of the 'Hell's Kettles', which, in alliterative fashion, he described as: 'Sable, solemn, still and sulphurous'. But in his writings he also recalled the lingering memory with which he was left, following a visit to the site: 'There was something about these pits, nevertheless, unearthly and solemn, producing an effect upon the mind, peculiar and lasting.'

And of course it is still said, though perhaps less frequently now, that on a fine day, if you stare long enough, you can, even today, see the lost farmer driving his horses and his cart full of hay, down in the clear water, many fathoms deep.

The King, the Mayor and the Bishop's Beer

Hugh Wright had been appointed as the first ever Mayor of Durham in 1602, when Queen Elizabeth I was still on the throne of England.

The city was beginning to acquire a civic identity of its own, independent of the incumbent Prince Bishop. A charter for a market, with freedoms for its traders, had originally been granted by Prince Bishop Hugh of Le Puiset in 1179; the charter was later confirmed by Papal Bull, the only one of its kind in the country and successive bishops had granted more and more freedom to the tradesmen and civic worthies of the city.

However, not all Prince Bishops shared this 'enlightened' view and not all shared the expanding vision of the merchant classes of Durham, for they had their own rights, which had been jealously guarded since Norman times. Relations between City and Bishop were sometimes tense, sometimes hostile, and when, in 1617, King James I visited Durham on his way to his native Scotland, he could not have known that he would be walking into what proved to be something of a storm in a beer mug.

James had first visited the city of Durham in 1603, the year of his Coronation, following the death of Queen Elizabeth. The histories record that he entered by Framwellgate Bridge and after regally ascending Silver Street, he was met in the Market Place by the new Mayor of Durham, James Farrales, and by the entire Corporation 'in all the glory of their new livery'. The entourage then passed up Saddler Street to the castle where the King was received and royally entertained by the Bishop, the witty and urbane Toby Matthew, and, as a traditional act of clemency from a new monarch, the King signed a royal warrant for the release of certain prisoners then in captivity in the city.

Fourteen years later, in the springtime, King James returned north again. His passage through the bishopric was, so the chronicles record, 'a local event of considerable interest'. And, on Maundy Thursday, he was lodged at the Bishop's Palace of Auckland Castle. In Durham City, this year's Mayor, George Walton, and his Corporation, were in deep discussion about the state of affairs with the current Bishop, William James.

James had succeeded Toby Matthew but he had not shown the same liberal acceptance of the freedoms granted to the traders of Durham as his predecessor had in his own charter. Bishop James, so they claimed, was trying to do the opposite, to curtail those freedoms and to take back ancient rights for his own. Trouble had started back in 1609, and now it was coming to a head.

Against this background, a letter was delivered to the Mayor from Auckland Castle. It was from the King, stating that, in two days time, he would proceed on a 'State visit' to the city. Preparations were hurriedly made, for this was a chance to demonstrate to the King himself the forward thinking ways of the ancient city and the desire for trade expansion, so earnestly wished for by an enlightened Corporation. It was also a chance, not to be missed, to make their case to the King against a draconian prelate.

On 18th April the King arrived. This time he and his retinue entered the city from the east where he was met on Elvet Bridge by George Walton, on horseback and surrounded by his aldermen. It is to be wondered whether he knew what he was walking into. Walton made a generous speech of welcome. However, he failed not in an early opportunity to take a swipe at the attitude and recent actions of the Bishop, stressing that, since medieval times, this was a 'City enabled with divers liberties and privilages'.

He went on to remind the King that all sovereignty in matters temporal and spiritual resided in him; and as the King had previously re-granted their former civic liberties and had them confirmed under the Great Seal of England, the rights and privileges of the city were for him, and him alone, to give or to take away. After this somewhat pointed diatribe, Walton presented the King with what some have recorded as a silver bowl, and others a golden cup, in honour of his visit.

From Elvet Bridge, the Mayor led King James in procession to the Market Place, where he was subjected to another speech, this time a well rehearsed piece, recited by an apprentice. Once again it is said, the verses 'cleverly hinted' at the resentment of the Bishop felt by the traders of the city.

Clearly, and not very subtly, the Corporation were attempting to gain the favour of the King, or at least were trying to ensure his good wishes, to get him on their side, in their ongoing dispute with the Bishop:

> *Durham's old City thus salutes our King!*
> *Which entertainment she doth humbly bring;*
> *For the great Prelate which of late adored,*
> *Her dignities, and for which we implored*
> *Your Highness' aid to have continuance …*

So said the apprentice; indeed there were verses of this stuff, and as the young speaker was drawing to a close, the real barb was saved for the last few lines:

> *There is one seeks our undoing, but to you*
> *Ten thousand hearts shall pray, and knees shall bow*
>
> *Confirm our Grant, good King, Durham's old City,*
> *Would be more powerful so it had James's pity.*

We are told that: 'the King made no recorded response to the effusion of the Corporation.' What he was actually thinking is anyone's guess. But now it was the Bishop's turn to curry favour with his monarch. So the King and his entourage were led up Saddler Street, first to the cathedral, and then to the castle, there to spend the next few days as a guest of the Bishop.

The real mystery of the story is what happened during the King's stay with Bishop James. Something clearly went wrong for the prelate, as it is related that, before his departure on 24th April, 'The King took the Bishop aside and soundly rated him.'

Had the King, it is to be wondered, some sympathy with the Mayor and Corporation, and their frustration at the limitations imposed by the Bishop on the expansion of their trade? Or had he simply vented his fury on Bishop James for being allowed to be subjected to the impertinent, self-serving diatribe of the city's traders? Perhaps, even, he was angry that the Bishop had taken it upon himself to obstruct or even to reverse civic rights, granted by charter and confirmed under the royal hand.

More mundanely, however, but perhaps more likely, it has been suggested that the King's anger was brought about by some failure of courtesy in the Bishop's household. Bishop James had a reputation for being rather a dull, dreary man, in sharp contrast to his predecessor. He was also mean with his money, frugal in his habits and somewhat parsimonious with his entertainment. Some have even said, perhaps apocryphally, that the real reason for the King's wrath was the lack of froth on his beer. The beer, it was said, being served to him by the Bishop whilst still too 'new', and not at all to his liking.

Perhaps then it was the combination of a dull host, poor entertainment and bad beer that had caused the King to chastise Bishop James. But whatever the real reason, the Bishop took it so badly, it was said, that he suddenly fell ill and within three weeks he was dead.

Intriguingly, the Bishop's funeral took place at night, apparently to avoid hostile demonstrations by the public. And for night after night afterwards, there were riots throughout the city and threats of damage to the Bishop's property in protest against the actions of the late, if not lamented prelate. Even the Church Histories, never normally wanting in fulsome praise for past prelates, simply record, 'William James, held the See eleven years, during which time nothing very remarkable occurred, he died in 1617.'

Justice Ettrick and the Duke of Baubleshire

William Ettrick was a Sunderland magistrate of the late 18th century. He was well known for being upright, impartial, and quite eccentric. At home, he lived quietly at High Barnes, the large house and estate that he'd inherited from his father. In his courtroom, however, he presided for many years, 'in all the plenitude of magisterial dignity'.

On more than one occasion he sat in judgement upon himself. Once, a local farmer appeared in front of Ettrick, accused of sending his cart to market without his name being painted on it, as the law required. The farmer pleaded ignorance of that particular law but was reminded severely by the magistrate of the old legal maxim: 'Ignorance of the Law is no excuse!' He was fined seven shillings and sixpence and left the court, a disgruntled man.

Making his way home, he happened to notice Ettrick's own dung cart, carrying manure from the fish quay to High Barnes Farm. He also happened to notice that Ettrick's dung cart did not have his name written upon it; whereupon the vengeful farmer rushed back to the scene of his recent punishment. Justice Ettrick was dutifully appraised of what the farmer had seen and decided immediately to sit in judgement upon himself. After due consideration of the facts in the overwhelming case against him, he found himself guilty and fined himself the same amount as he had the now triumphant farmer.

But Ettrick's eccentricities were not confined to the courtroom. Although never having taken part in the 'Sport' himself, he once issued a challenge to a champion prizefighter, newly arrived in the district. The pugilist, perhaps unsurprisingly not wishing to lay violent hands on the town's chief magistrate, made his excuses and left. Upon hearing of his actions, Ettrick exclaimed, 'Tell him from me that he is a great coward.'

And so his life passed and throughout his years he remained something of a curiosity. He loved to write verse, although as the chroniclers record, 'it would have been a misuse of terms to call him a poet'. Even at his death, aged 83, he showed a talent for the peculiar. For in his will he left the bizarre instructions that his body be 'carried in my dung cart to the grave' there to be 'buried at or about the hour of twelve of the clock at night'. So ended the term of William Ettrick, the Sunderland magistrate. In Durham City, however, eccentricity was not merely the preserve of the legal profession but of the nobility too; though nobility of questionable pedigree.

James Brown had originally been the owner of a rag shop and the self-styled 'Poet Laureate of Newcastle' moved to Durham City, after the death of his first wife. Throughout the rest of his life, Brown was notorious for writing dubious verse, usually of a religious, apocalyptic nature, his poems having, it was said, 'neither rhyme nor reason'. But that mattered not to Brown, who declared that the Archangel Gabriel had both seen and approved his work. He was also convinced that he would never die and would ascend into heaven visibly. But James Brown P.L., as he always signed himself, was also *uncommonly susceptible to flattery*' and therefore easy prey for the perpetrators of practical jokes. When, aged 90, he received in the post, a Patent of Nobility, creating him 'Baron Brown of Durham', he considered it well overdue; and the chronicles tell that he 'never detected the imposture'. But even the Baron Bard was outranked, both in nobility and in eccentricity, by another titled contemporary, the Duke of Baubleshire.

Sometimes, when out and about, we've all probably experienced the embarrassment of bumping into someone that we know but don't really want to talk to. We are no doubt familiar with that sinking feeling when they 'heave to' into an unavoidable sight line and the depressing inevitability hits that avoidance is no longer an option.

Then, of course, there are the complete strangers who decide to open random conversations, which you quickly realise are either just a little odd, not really relevant to anything you are doing or anything that is happening around you, or that are simply deluded. And your desire for a speedy conclusion to the discourse is matched only by your desire to put a safe distance between yourself and this strange person. Such people, however, are not just a product of 21st-century County Durham.

Durham City has never been short of 'characters', whether in kind like those alluded to above, or others, perhaps more outrageous. The

exploits and idiosyncrasies of some of these 'characters' would even be considered worthy of remembrance in the histories of Durham, becoming over time, a part of the legendary fabric of the city itself.

Thomas French was one of these characters. In fact he was described in the Victorian *Monthly Chronicle of North Country Lore and Legend*, not just as a Durham character, but as a Durham institution.

Not much is known about French before he rose to his imagined station, except that he was believed to have been an industrious and honest working man. It is sympathetically recorded in the chronicles that he 'Assumed his Title' entirely of his own accord 'with the decline of his understanding' and he began to adorn himself daily with all the trappings of the nobility. A coloured paper star worn on the breast of his coat served as the insignia of a noble chivalric order, known only to him. A paper cockade in his hat added perhaps an indication of the highest military rank and we are told that a 'liberal display of brass curtain rings on his fingers complemented his outfit'.

And so it was that Thomas French received his aristocratic sobriquet; and resplendent in his curious garb, the Duke of Baubleshire began to promenade the streets of St Cuthbert's city.

And here he spent his time accosting passers-by, generally people he knew, but he was always glad of new company, and subjecting them to the benefit of his wisdom and noble station. No topic was beyond him: business was a favourite, especially the interests of the extensive Baubleshire estates. And he would insist that he was the constant victim of fraud that had cost him dearly in cash and bank bills.

When seeing a valuable horse or a fine expensive carriage pass along the street or draw up in the Market Place, he would, to all present, claim it as his; a claim which he would insist upon, often berating the rightful owner, regardless of rank or social standing and accusing them of misappropriation. Naturally enough this led to him being 'exceedingly annoying to the possessors of the property in dispute'. However, for the onlookers in the city, it no doubt enlivened more than one dull day.

But regardless of, or perhaps because of, his idiosyncrasies, he was generally accepted and tolerated with good humour by the citizens of Durham. By and large they enjoyed his company and were amused by his stories and disclosures about his frequent and intimate correspondence with King George III, on the subjects of war, foreign possessions and other important affairs of state.

Often the Duke of Baubleshire publicly proclaimed his title to immense possessions 'though at no time being master of a shilling', and he died, aged 85, in the workhouse of Durham City, on 16th May 1796. Such had been his fame, however, that a lithographed portrait had been published before his death and he would be further immortalised, though slightly mockingly, by a contemporary poet, from whose lines the following are taken:

> *Through Durham daily he took his walk,*
> *And talk'd, 'ye gods, how he could talk'*
> *His private riches, how immense!*
> *His Public Virtue, how intense!*
> *Pre-eminent of all the Great,*
> *His mighty wisdom rules the State!*

But perhaps, reader, if we, whilst out and about in Durham, were to have bumped into his Grace, he would not have engendered in us the same feelings of horror brought about by those alluded to earlier. Perhaps if the duke 'hove to' into unavoidable contact and discourse, we would simply have smiled resignedly and asked him about the state of the city, or of the government, or of the monarchy; and passed a few minutes in his gentle, amusing, alternative world.

Murder on the Moors

This story is set in the middle of the 18th century, during the days of lead mining in the Durham Dales. For their subsistence, the lead miners were paid a small monthly sum of money by the mine owners but the main settlement was paid annually in accordance with the 'bargain' agreed between them and paid against how much lead ore the miners had actually dug from the earth. Consequently the annual 'pay' was a notable event, with most miners suddenly having disposable income: debts could be paid, necessities could be bought, even small luxuries could be afforded.

Of course, the availability of such disposable income also attracted those happy to assist in its disposal, and an influx of itinerant travellers, tradesmen, peddlars and other, perhaps less honest individuals, made their way into the more remote areas of the Durham Dales. But the wild moors over which they had to come could be crossed only with difficulty and danger lay before those who did not know the way. It was a custom therefore that travellers hired local guides to see them safely from one lonely place to another. However, the more visiting tradesmen that appeared in the Dales, then the fewer the available guides to keep them safe on their journeys.

The subject of this tale is a traveller, who, having made an excellent profit by selling to the lead miners of Alston, Nenthead and Allendale, arrived with his wares in Weardale. After further good business, witnessed by a promisingly bulging money bag, he wished to cross the bleak uplands that would take him south into Teesdale. The road that needed to be taken was rough, deeply rutted and crossed occasionally by deep pools of water that had strayed from the upland streams and torrents that drained the lonely expanse of the high moors. Few travellers went that way. In 1327 a whole Scots army had simply melted away over the same route and disappeared from the pursuing English. Our lone traveller tried therefore to procure a guide, but to no avail. He was well aware, however, that to remain ahead of the competition, he must get to Teesdale as quickly as possible, so he mounted his horse and set off across the moors alone.

The going was rough and dangerous; it was certainly a road less travelled by the local population and used only when necessity demanded. Bounded at first by menacing high hedges, it eventually gave out onto the open desolate moorland. It was a landscape that lent its reputation easily to dread stories of robbers and outlaws, lying in wait behind lonely rocky outcrops or deep within the scattered shadowy stands of pine trees, which whispered their menace in the swirling night air. It was also said that this was the abode of the unquiet spirits of the dead, whose tortured cries could be heard, carried on the wailing moorland winds. So it was with hope and more than a little trepidation that our traveller set out on his journey – 'he was alone, in a strange place, on a gloomy road, and in charge of a large sum of money'. And he was last seen, at least in earthly form, near a tract of farmland called Park House Pasture; after that 'by what drear road he passed to eternity is unknown'.

A farmhouse stood hard by Park House Pasture and it was the resident farmer whose sleep was disturbed in the night. He was startled from his shallow slumbers by terrifying sounds coming from the direction of a field to the rear of his house. This was a lonely, isolated spot and both he and his family were familiar with wild night-time cries from the resident members of the animal kingdom. But these cries he had not heard before and at first superstition and imagination gave life to some dread, dark creatures from a very different world.

A second time he heard them, but this time they were fainter and he recognised now, with some relief, that they were made, after all, by a human voice; but to his returning alarm, he at once realised they were clearly therefore the cries of someone in some extreme and violent distress. He listened further as the dreadful sounds gradually faded and fell silent, perhaps being blown away by the wind or, perhaps, like a lost and tormented soul, being carried off by the darkness and the night. Undaunted, the old farmer, though frail and bent, determined to sally forth into the darkness and solve the mystery. His wife and daughter, however, thought better of it and after much coaxing and persuasion, the old man was convinced to wait until the safety of the morning before commencing his investigation. So it was that at first light he rose, dressed and headed off in the direction of the previous night's disturbance.

What he found compounded the mystery. The pasture was pitted with hoof marks but these particular hoof marks did not speak of the terror of a Satanic visitation; the old man knew well that they had been made by a horse. But of the horse that had made them, or of its rider, there was no trace. There was no spilled blood, nor indeed any signs of the foul play that would have explained those terrible night-time cries; simply wild and heavy hoof prints in a wet and muddy field. The pasture was enclosed on all sides by high hedges and at only one place, where a gate stood, was there an exit. This gate opened onto a narrow track, with another gate directly opposite. But the gate in the hedge, the only means of exiting the pasture, was closed and securely tied, preventing any egress from the field. What had happened the previous night could not be guessed, and the participants in whatever weird drama had taken place there had, it seemed, simply vanished into thin air.

So what had actually happened that dark night near Park House Pasture could not be ascertained. The lone traveller was never seen again. Together, in the eyes of the local population, the two mysteries quickly became two acts in the same drama. With absolutely no evidence to support their theory, the locals were convinced that the dread screams heard by the farmer had been the last earthly sounds made by the man. Both he and his horse, they were convinced, had been spirited away by someone, or something, bent on murder, or worse. However, not too much time had elapsed before suspicions were aroused of a decidedly earthbound explanation for the event. An explanation that, it seemed, confirmed the theory of the local people. It was reported that three men had been seen acting suspiciously in the vicinity. One of the men, it was reported, had even been seen leading a horse down some nearby old mine workings. It was further alleged that these three mystery men suddenly began to throw around a deal of money, as if they had come into some fortune.

At last it was clear what must have happened! These itinerant three had waylaid the unfortunate traveller in the night, in the field near Park House Pasture, murdered him, taken his money and hidden his horse until it could be quietly sold on without arousing any suspicion. Enquiries were subsequently made but absolutely nothing was found. The three reported ne'er-do-wells seemingly vanished, and neither the horse nor the body of the allegedly murdered traveller were ever found.

And so there the mystery lay. And where there is mystery, there usually follows legend. Rumours began to circulate, whispers of a terrifying presence that appeared in the dead of night near Park House Pasture: the visitation of the spectre of the murdered traveller, covered in the blood of his death wounds and mounted upon his terrifying phantom horse, which careered wildly over the field before disappearing before the very eyes of the horror-struck witness. Such was the tale of the ghost of the lost traveller of Weardale, which, over the years that followed, became a staple both of fireside and ale house.

At the beginning of the 19th century, a new road was cut through land near Park House Pasture. On excavating for the foundations, workmen came across a curious thing: the skeleton of a man, buried, rather oddly, in an upright position. The skeleton was found not very far from the spot where, so many years before, the old farmer had been disturbed by those terrifying cries in the night.

Sanctuary

*The Sanctuary Knocker, circa 1140 – Cast Bronze, Lion's Head,
has a tendril-like mane protruding from behind the face. The
Knocker represents, in three dimensional form, the beasts depicted in
the St. Calais manuscripts.*

The Treasures of Saint Cuthbert

The year was 1487. Adam Ewbank was alone and a fugitive on the
wild, bleak moors that separated the County Palatine of Durham
from Cumberland. He was following the line of the old Roman road,
past the site of the Rey Cross, the spot, so the chronicles tell, where,
in AD 954, Eric Bloodaxe, the last Viking king of York, was slain in
battle. But Ewbank had no time to dally and muse about those that
had come this way before; he was fleeing eastward, towards Durham
and he was in haste.

Five years before, Rowland Mebburne, a parson from Wycliffe on
the River Tees, not far from Barnard Castle, had turned his face north
and made his own journey to St Cuthbert's city. Three years after him,
James Manfield, also from Wycliffe, followed in Mebburne's footsteps.
And in 1491 Thomas Spence of Bowes travelled the eastward route
previously taken by Adam Ewbank.

All these men made their fateful journeys to Durham to claim the
Right of Sanctuary at the Shrine of St Cuthbert, for they were all
killers. Ewbank had slain a man on Stainmore, and he rang the
sanctuary bell in Durham Cathedral on 10th October 1487.
Mebburne, the parson, had attacked a man with a knife and, piercing
his heart, had killed him. Thomas Spence, with the aid of another,
had hanged an innocent Scotsman. And James Manfield had
committed murder in a revenge killing. For three of these men, their
fate would be banishment from the kingdom of England. The other
would die.

It is said that it was King Alfred the Great who first ruled that 'St.
Cuthbert's Church should be a safe sanctuary for all fugitives'.

Apparently St Cuthbert had appeared to him in a dream, 'holding a gospel book ornamented with Gold and gems', and had given the beleaguered King the strength to achieve final victory in his wars against the Danes. And so it was that Durham Cathedral, with its almost mystical power as the guardian of the Shrine of St Cuthbert, would remain until Tudor times one of the main places of refuge in the north of England. There is even an instance of one Robert Marshall claiming sanctuary for the highest offence of treason against the King, and the King acknowledging by letter the sanctity of his protection at Durham.

In previous centuries, the Anglo-Saxon kings had held the Right of Sanctuary as inviolate and those who followed the Anglo-Saxons – the Viking King Cnut and William the Conqueror's Norman dynasty – all confirmed the right at Durham. We are told that in the 12th century, during the episcopacy of Prince Bishop Hugh of Le Puiset, the city was surrounded at a distance of about a mile in each direction by a number of crosses, or sanctuary posts, defining the limits of Durham's right of sanctuary. However, by the 15th century, fugitives fleeing from the law would have to reach either the cathedral or the cathedral yard before being able to claim their safety.

When the breathless fugitive had swung the sanctuary knocker, and its hollow call had echoed through the massive building, two monks who, it is claimed, were permanently on watch, day and night, in a chamber overlooking the north door, would descend and let him in. On claiming the protection of the Church, he would be taken to the Galilee Chapel, where the sanctuary bell would be tolled, to let it be known that someone had claimed the right. The offender would then be required first to declare before witnesses his offence and then to toll the sanctuary bell himself, in token of his request.

The felon would then be stripped of his clothes, which would be passed to the sacrist as a fee, and given a black gown with a yellow cross of St Cuthbert embroidered on the left shoulder, indicating his status. He was now under the protection of the Church. An alcove, near the south door of the Galilee Chapel, enclosed by an iron grille, would be his refuge and his shelter. Here he would remain for thirty-seven days, during which time he would be supplied with food, drink and bedclothes by the monks of Durham, and within that time he was required to appear before the coroner, to confess his crime and 'Abjure the Realm', swearing on the Gospels that in return for avoiding trial and execution he would leave England and never come back.

After his period under the protection of the Church, he would leave, carrying before him a rough, white-painted wooden cross, tied together with a rope, and normally in the care of the under-sheriff who then passed him from constable to constable, until he reached the designated port, Hartlepool, then the seaport of the Prince Bishop. On pain of death, he could neither leave the road, nor stay in one place for more than one night. Anyone giving him food or shelter after the period of the Church's protection would themselves be punished as felons. On reaching Hartlepool he was required to take the first ship leaving the shores of England, regardless of its destination. If there was no such ship in the harbour, he was required to wade into the sea every day, as testimony of his oath to leave, until such time as a ship did sail away.

In reality, however, many abjurers probably never made it to foreign shores. Some would be waylaid on route to the port and murdered in revenge by relatives or friends of their victims. Others would simply abscond and melt away into the forests and the wild to become 'Wolfshead', there to live the rest of their lives outside of the law, not subject to the law and not protected by it; to be treated as was the wolf, which anyone was justly entitled to hunt, capture and dispatch.

From the reign of King Henry VIII, all fugitives abjuring the realm were, before leaving, branded on the right thumb with the letter 'A' to ensure that if they tried to return, they would be revealed for what they were and would receive an immediate sentence of death. But, in practice, the Right of Sanctuary began to be eroded in Tudor times as it was seen to be abused, regarded by criminals simply as a method of avoiding the scrutiny of a jury. A man named Colson, a thief from Wolsingham in Weardale, escaped from the prison in which he'd been incarcerated and immediately made his way straight to Durham Cathedral, there to claim St Cuthbert's protection and avoid recapture. And, of course, those claiming sanctuary, were required to abjure only the realm of England. There are stories of Scottish border raiders, bandits and cattle thieves, who, with capture looking inevitable, deliberately claimed sanctuary and the protection of the Church, abjuring the realm of England and eventually making their way back to Scotland to start all over again.

So it was that, in 1531, Abjuration of the Realm was abolished. All forms of treason were withdrawn from the Right of Sanctuary and there was a general attempt to remove the Church's automatic protection of criminals. Thomas Cromwell, Chief Minister of Henry VIII, drew up a list of eight towns in England that would instead serve as specific centres of sanctuary. There was much opposition to his plan, NIMBYism, Tudor-style, the residents of the selected towns, perhaps understandably, being unwilling to allow their communities to be safe havens for criminals.

But the Right of Sanctuary in a church had always been strongly supported by the clergy as a means to protect the weak from the strong, the unpopular from the mob, and the common man who had, for some reason or other, displeased the local lord. So much so that when, in 1378, Ralph Ferrars, a retainer of the immensely powerful John of Gaunt, Duke of Lancaster and third son of King Edward III, had forced his way into Westminster Abbey, slain a man and carried off his compatriot to prison, both of whom were under the protection of Sanctuary, Ferrars and all who had aided him were excommunicated by the Archbishop of Canterbury, and 'Dammed in the eyes of God'.

On her accession to the throne in 1553, Mary Tudor attempted to restore in full the privileges of Sanctuary, but she was dead before this happened and her younger stepsister, Elizabeth I, would place further limits on the ancient rights. Finally, in 1624, an Act of King James I abolished the age-old privilege, which had been recognised in England as far back as the 9th century, with the rather prosaic words, 'Be it also enacted, that no sanctuary or privilege of sanctuary shall hereafter be allowed in any case.'

So what then did fate have in store for our own fugitives? Both Adam Ewbank and Thomas Spence successfully claimed the Sanctuary of St Cuthbert's church and, as far as is known, went into exile. The Parson of Wycliffe, Rowland Mebburne, who had stabbed to death a man named Robert Manfield, was pardoned by the King and released. Three years later, however, one James Manfield, with the assistance of others, attacked Mebburne in the village of Ovington, not far from Wycliffe, piercing his body with a 'Wallych Bill' and giving him 'a mortal hurt of which he incontinently died'. And so, on 25th February 1485, Manfield himself arrived in front of the sanctuary knocker at Durham Cathedral and claimed the protection of St Cuthbert until the time came for his own exile.

And so also began perhaps, according to the Rev James Raine, writing in 1815, a local story, familiar to him since childhood. He remembered that the people of Ovington village had lived in fear of a spectre, often seen in a field at the edge of a wood, on the road between Ovington and Wycliffe. The shade was that of a priest robed in a gown of rustling silk, 'with respect to whose name or cause of restlessness, no tradition had been preserved', the Rev Raine tells us. But perhaps it was the ghost of the murderer Rowland Mebburne, who in life was released from the sanctuary of St Cuthbert by order of the King, only to be murdered, in turn, at the vengeful hand of James Manfield.

So a sanctuary knocker still glowers out from the great north door of Durham Cathedral, as it probably has done since the year 1140. Between 1464 and 1524, three hundred and thirty-one souls claimed their right. We know that the hands of Rowland Mebburne, James Manfield, Adam Ewbank and Thomas Spence all grasped the smooth bronze handle that hung from the lion's mouth and hammered out their claim. These were the hands of desperate men, the hands of fugitives from the law, the hands of killers. But how many other hands, it is to be wondered, did the same; for the right existed from the days of the Anglo-Saxons, until the last time the hollow hammering of the sanctuary knocker was heard at Durham, on 10th September 1524. Records show that they were by no means all local men, they came from as far afield as Lincolnshire, Northamptonshire and from Derbyshire. There were among their numbers mainly murderers, a hundred and ninety-five of them, but there were also horse thieves, cattle rustlers and burglars. Their exact number, however, will probably never be known, as before 1464 no records were kept.

The sanctuary knocker we see hanging on the north door of Durham Cathedral today, that vision of 'some monstrous beast, unknown save in the literature and art of fabledom', is a replica; the 12th-century original can be seen inside, in its rightful place amongst the Treasures of St Cuthbert. The replica knocker is only thirty years old, and on its completion, in celebration of the modern-day craftsman's art, and as part of a lesson for schoolchildren about the ancient Right of Sanctuary, both knockers were shown together, side by side, on an edition of the children's TV programme *Blue Peter*, prompting an unfortunate, presumably accidental and often re-broadcast gaffe by the admiring, but ultimately red-faced presenter, who summed up the piece by opining what a magnificent pair they were!

Bibliography

Andrews, W. (Ed) *Bygone Durham*, 1898

Brockie, W. *Legends and Superstitions of the County of Durham*, 1886

Denham, M.A. *The Denham Tracts*, 1846–1859

Dodd, James J. *The History of the Urban District of Spennymoor*, 1897

Fordyce, W. *The History and Antiquities of the County Palatine of Durham*, 1855–1857

Grice, F. *Folk Tales of the North Country*, 1944

Hutchinson, W. *The History and Antiquities of the County Palatine of Durham*: 1785–1794

Low, J.L. *Diocesan Histories – Durham*, 1881

Longstaffe, W.H.D. *The History and Antiquities of the Parish of Darlington*, 1854

Mackenzie, E. & Ross, M. *An Historical, Topographical and Descriptive View of the County of Durham*, 1834

The Monthly Chronicle of North Country Lore and Legend, 1887–1890

Ramsden, M. *Teesdale*, 1947

Richardson, M.A. *The Local Historian's Table Book of Remarkable Occurrences*, 1841–1846

Surtees, R. *The History and Antiquities of the County Palatine of Durham*, 1816–1823; 1840

Sharp, Sir Cuthbert *A list of the Knights and Burgesses who have represented the County and City of Durham*, 1826

Sharp, Sir Cuthbert *Memorials of the Rebellion of 1569*, 1840

Sykes, J. *Local Records: Historical Register of Remarkable Events*, 1824–1833

The Victoria History of the Counties of England *A History of Durham*, 1928 Ed.

Watson, R. *The Poetical Works of Richard Watson*, 1884